LUCILE Ltd

LONDON, PARIS,

NEW YORK and CHICAGO

1890s – 1930s

LUCILE Ltd

LONDON, PARIS,

NEW YORK and CHICAGO

1890s – 1930s

By VALERIE D. MENDES and AMY DE LA HAYE

V&A Publishing

First published by V&A Publishing, 2009

V&A Publishing
Victoria and Albert Museum
South Kensington
London SW7 2RL

Distributed in North America by
Harry N. Abrams, Inc., New York

ISBN 978 1 851 77561 3
Library of Congress Control Number 2008937536
10 9 8 7 6 5 4 3 2 1
2013 2012 2011 2010 2009

A catalogue record for this book is
available from the British Library.

Book and cover design:
John and Orna Designs, London

Indexer:
Vicki Robinson

New V&A photography by Sara Hodges,
Ian Thomas and Richard Davies, V&A
Photographic Studio

Front jacket illustration:
Five watercolour designs from the album,
From Lucile Ltd. Autumn 1905.

Back jacket illustration:
Fabrics and trimmings from the design
'An Episode' framing a duster coat from
Spring 1918. Sample pages *From Lucile Ltd.
Autumn 1905*.

Frontispiece:
Fur-trimmed, silk velvet evening cloak
worn with dramatic, sculpted felt hat with
aigrette. Studio Lucile 1913-15.

Printed in China

V&A Publishing
Victoria and Albert Museum
South Kensington
London SW7 2RL
www.vam.ac.uk

LUCILE Ltd

Acknowledgements

Valerie D. Mendes and Amy de la Haye 2008

First and foremost we acknowledge the great generosity of the late Earl of Halsbury, FRS. His donation of the Lucile Archive to the Victoria and Albert Museum forms a permanent record of his grandmother's unique achievements and will prove an inspirational resource for generations to come. With typical kind-heartedness the late Earl encouraged this project and looked forward to its publication. We are sincerely grateful to his daughters, Lady Caroline Blois and Lady Clare Lindsay, for their enthusiastic support of the project, and to Elinor Glyn's daughter, the late Lady Juliet Rhys Williams.

This book was first mooted in the 1980s and resurfaced 20 years later. The V&A has been supportive throughout. The Furniture, Textiles and Fashion Department, led by Christopher Wilk, has sustained the authors and, in their busy schedule, many curators have been generous with their time and knowledge. We especially thank Sonnet Stanfill for her professionalism and generosity; Clare Browne for identifying the lace; Oriole Cullen for spotting the evening gown 'Carresaute'; Edwina Ehrman for facts about the Museum of London's Lucile collection; and Susan North, Daniel Milford-Cottam and Suzanne Smith for smoothing our path. We acknowledge Samantha Erin Safer who, diligently, and with growing affection for its contents, catalogued the Lucile Archive over a period of many months; kindly shared American magazine texts with us; and provided key appendices. It was a pleasure to work with Alexia Kirk of the Archive of Art and Design, Stephen Calloway and Moira Thunder of Prints and Drawings, and Cathy Haill of Theatre Collections – we are grateful to them for their valuable specialist advice. In the Textiles Conservation Department, Gill Owen painstakingly conserved the *Autumn 1905* album soon after its acquisition, and recently the Head of Furniture, Textiles and Fashion Conservation, Marion Kite, has directed conservation of Lucile material. In Publishing, Mary Butler calmly completed the preliminary stages before her retirement and subsequently Mark Eastment, Frances Ambler and Catherine Blake (with admirable patience and good humour) have steered us through all editorial intricacies. Designer Orna Frommer-Dawson's sensitive and creative response to Lucile's designs and working documents, combined with the exceptional talents of V&A photographers Sara Hodges, Ian Thomas and Richard Davis, have resulted in a publication that is noteworthy not only for its beauty and handle, but also for being absolutely 'right'. We are indebted to members of the V&A's National Art Library and Photographic Studio for their expertise.

Generous, as ever, Caroline Evans (Central Saint Martins) shared her American research with us, Al Rees (Royal College of Art) and Bryony Dixon (British Film Institute) gave us leads about Lucile's involvement with film, while Carly Eck carefully aided our search through newspapers and magazines. We thank librarians, archivists and curators in the British Library (including the Newspaper Library at Colindale), the Westminster Archive, the National Archive at Kew, Special Collections in the Hartley Library of the University of Southampton, Companies House, the London Library, Condé Nast (*Vogue*), The National Magazine Company Ltd (*Harper's Bazaar*) and London College of Fashion.

Valerie Mendes was tempted away from garden and travels to work with Amy de la Haye, and is grateful to friends, family and former museum colleagues for bearing with her. She particularly thanks Loraine Fletcher and, as ever, Peter Mendes, who kept her informed, fed and focused.

Amy de la Haye acknowledges the London College of Fashion, where she is Reader in Material Culture and Fashion Curation, and Joint Director of the MA in Fashion Curation with Judith Clark, an inspirational colleague and valued friend. To those most dear - Kevin, Felix and her parents, Brian and Julia - she offers heartfelt thanks.

OPPOSITE Detail of samples for evening gowns, Autumn 1905.

Introduction

Portrait of Lady Duff Gordon. An off-the-shoulder Lucile gown has layers of frilled lace and embroidered edgings with a delicate, loosely draped fichu tied beneath a central silk flower head. Set against this Edwardian frou-frou, the inclusion of a single chunky cross-shaped earring strikes a peculiarly modern note. Her luxuriant, slightly dishevelled auburn hair is worn up in a winged style and a pearl *sautoir* is wound around her neck. With hands clasped, Lucile stares straight at the camera with a slightly apprehensive expression. Bassano Studio, 1904. The National Portrait Gallery, London

Lady Duff Gordon – 'Lucile', as she was known – had justifiable confidence in her considerable talents as a fashion designer and dressmaker. Throughout her long career she approached the profession's complexities with admirable tenacity and vigour. In addition to the distinctive Lucile style, her innovative modes of presentation, adept reading of the fashion market and astute preservation of designs – laced with a lively propensity for self-publicity – have all played a part in securing her legacy. Her diverse achievements have been recognized in the press and by numerous fashion and theatre historians and curators, while her luxurious clothes are housed in museum collections worldwide.

This monograph is devoted to Lucile as designer and maker of fashionable clothes, highlighting artefacts from the Victoria and Albert Museum's collection of her work. It centres upon a rare fashion album, *From Lucile Ltd. Autumn 1905,* which contains painstakingly executed watercolours and pasted-in fabric samples – miniature summaries of the fabrics and trimmings used in each ensemble. This project offered an opportunity to extend the narrative by examining works contained within the Lucile Archive (including drawings, photographs and press cuttings), which Lucile's grandson, the late Earl of Halsbury FRS, carefully preserved and most generously presented to the V&A in the 1960s. The Lucile Archive, catalogued by Samantha Erin Safer, is located in the Museum's Archive of Art & Design.

Lucile nomenclature is somewhat confusing. Born Lucy Christiana Sutherland, she apparently detested her first name (though extended to 'Lucile', it was destined to become famous as the title of her fashion enterprise), and it appears that her intimate friends knew her as Christiana. She became Mrs James Wallace on her first marriage in 1884 and Lady Duff Gordon on her second marriage in 1900. Initially she operated as 'Mrs Lucy Wallace' but by the early 1890s was also using the title 'Maison Lucile', then, very briefly, she called the business 'Madame Lucile'. Eventually Lucile (frequently misspelt 'Lucille') prevailed – it became a limited company in 1904 and thenceforward the names Lady Duff Gordon and Lucile were interchangeable.

Lucile's appearance, along with her personal and business affairs, were frequently recorded in newsprint. In March 1895 fashion journalist 'A' (probably the prolific fashion writer and editor, Mrs Aria) related her encounter with the then fledgling dressmaker in her premises in Old Burlington Street for *The Queen*: 'I went, I saw, and I was conquered… She showed me such a pretty bodice she was designing with her own fair hands, and a box of pins, made of shot chiné gauze, with a black ground mounted over a shot silk, with the yoke formed of iridescent sequins and glittering beads… There is a lovely assortment of fine lawn, with braid lace appliquéd upon it, which is being used to form blouses, fronts, and all sorts of delightful trifles which, light as air, make the sum of woman's costume. Mrs Wallace, *je vous salue.*' The foundations for an international business with a unique signature style had been laid. From this date until the early 1920s, designs by the dressmaker who was to gain international renown as Lucile were featured extensively in ladies' papers and fashion magazines, including *The Queen*, American *Good Housekeeping* and *Harper's Bazaar*, and British *Vogue*. A photograph of her, in ruffled lace and chiffon with a lapful of roses (her favourite flowers) formed the cover of *The Bystander* (15 June 1904) with the explanation: 'As Madame Lucile Lady Duff Gordon has achieved a position among the leading modistes of the day'. On 11 December 1904, in a regular column delightfully titled 'Between Sips of Tea', *The New York Times* offered a pen picture of Lucile: '…she has a pale complexion, piquant features, and is original and lively'. 'Original' is a term that was regularly applied to Lucile's designs and business innovations.

ABOVE An early version of the Lucile logo (1904). Lucile was entranced by 18th-century decorative arts. Her interiors and their furnishings – often achieved in collaboration with the interior designer Elsie de Wolfe – reflected this fascination. The Lucile insignia, with copper-plate style signature, festoons of beribboned rose stems and myrtle tendrils, reflected her taste for the romantic. The emblem was a neat advertising device (although Lucile very rarely bought advertising space), and it appeared in a number of variations in Lucile publications and theatre programmes.

OPPOSITE Full-length portrait of Lady Duff Gordon. Used for Lucile Ltd publicity purposes, this studio photograph captures the petite designer in a fur-edged, satin coat worn open over a pale, slender gown, below which peep tiny pointed court shoes. Her hair is worn up, wound around the head and she has the same *sautoir* of pearls shown in the 1904 portrait by Bassano. In *Hearth and Home* (November 1912), Lucile was described as being dainty and harmonious with a slight figure, while *The New York Times* (12 May 1912) stated: 'She is a fair creation, daintily chiselled, graceful in movement, arresting in speech.' Lallie Charles, *c.*1912

LADY DUFF GORDON

Mrs Constance Peel, fashion journalist and author, remembered Lucile as '…a pretty, graceful little woman with a talent for designing dresses and making them.'[1] This summary is significant as it reveals how Lucile was in control of the whole creative process, from initial concept to finished garment at a time when '…it was an unheard of thing that a lady should earn money with her needle' (*The Lady's Realm,* July 1898). While it was customary for aspiring dressmakers to learn their skills working as an apprentice within the industry or by studying at trade school, Lucile was self-taught and started as an independent. By 1909, she had transformed her small-scale London dressmaking concern into a sophisticated fashion house resembling a French couture establishment with its various ateliers, skilled hands, *cabine de mannequins, vendeuses* and luxurious *salon de vente.* Clothes with a Lucile label were custom-made (involving the usual fittings) by an in-house workforce. She invariably described herself as a dressmaker though when the Paris branch opened in 1910, she deemed herself a '*grande couturière*',[2] avoiding the word '*haute*' that might have incensed the Paris Chambre Syndicale de la Couture, with its strict rules governing an elite membership.

As early as 1928, Paul Nystrom, economist and Professor of Marketing at Columbia University, wrote in his *Economics of Fashion*: 'Her work has been marked by originality in sales promotion as well as artistic effects in apparel.' In her guide to style and taste, *This Age of Beauty*, the Hon. Mrs C.W. Forester, fashion journalist and author, acknowledged one of fashion's debts to Lucile: 'To her we owe the first conception of a dressmaker's shop as a *salon*, the social meeting place for a genuine aristocratic and artistic clientele. In many ways the advent of Lucille [*sic*] was a landmark in the history of modern beauty.' As the book was published in 1935, the year Lucile died, it is unlikely she had the gratification of reading this tribute. Autobiographies by friends, clients and fellow creative spirits, such as 'Daisy', Countess of Warwick, Lady Angela Forbes, Irene Castle and Howard Greer, offer diverse insights into Lucile's oeuvre, working practice, society clients and milieu.

Lucile appears to have orchestrated mainly happy establishments and, on the whole, her workforce remained remarkably faithful. Within her branches she controlled design and the many aspects of construction rigorously. A perfectionist, she obsessed over every detail and admitted that 'a gown is never permitted to leave my establishment until it pleases me'.[3] This was at a privileged distance from the miseries of the unregulated 'sweated industries' which fed the burgeoning ready-to-wear market as well as some exclusive dressmakers. This deplorable state of affairs was documented in grim detail by 'The Daily News Sweated Industries Exhibition' in 1906, and while other newspapers and reformers fought the cause, it was many years before laws were introduced to stamp out exploitation and protect the workforce. The pitiful pay, dire living conditions, long hours and consequent ill health of outworkers were harsh realities that hardly impinged on Lucile Ltd.

Lucile was passionate about and devoted to her *métier*; a titled lady, she was a workaholic through choice. Throughout her long fashion career – spanning four decades – she had the foresight to amass and preserve her working drawings, prints and photographs, not an easy task when she was moving regularly between Paris, London and New York. Yet, as museologist Susan Pearce has observed, 'Objects act as reminders and confirmers of our identity… they seem to ease our movement through life and act as a medium of passage.'[4] Whether Lucile kept her records to ensure her place in history we cannot establish, although the desire to capture our life story as we grow older, and then to disperse our

possessions safely before our death, is not uncommon and would be in keeping with her penchant for self-promotion. In 1928 she gave the Museum of London copies of two Lucile gowns, made for the famous musical comedy actresses Miss Lily Elsie (in 1910) and Miss Gertie Millar (in 1911). In a letter to the Museum she tellingly asserts: 'I am proud to think that the work put into them is fit to rival the lovely workmanship of the eighteenth century as displayed in some of the dresses of Spitalfields' silks already in the Museum.'[5] Four years later her autobiography, *Discretions and Indiscretions*, was published. Perhaps inevitably in the quest for recognition, this inflates her achievements, and is frustratingly vague about dates, but provides an illuminating, at times poignant, document.

Since the 1960s, fashion curators, historians and biographers have provided fresh insights into Lucile Ltd and the life of its founder. In 1986 Meredith Etherington-Smith and Jeremy Pilcher threaded their way with consummate skill through the complex personal lives of sisters Lady Duff Gordon and Elinor Glyn for their biographical duet, *The It Girls*. The authors summarized the allure of the siblings: 'To their contemporaries they were fascinating because they embodied an entirely individual sense of heightened reality, whether in the way they dressed, in the way they decorated their surroundings, or in what they said, wrote or designed.' It is a fascination that endures today. Recent studies examine Lucile in her role as a theatrical costumier. Joel H. Kaplan and Shiela Stowell's *Theatre and fashion: Oscar Wilde to the Suffragettes* (1994) focuses on the mutually beneficial interplay between fashion and theatre, exploring the costuming

exploits of Lucile and many of her contemporaries. They discovered the popular novelist and journalist Marie Corelli's antipathetic response to Lucile's 'Private View to Costume Suggestions', April 1904: 'The whole thing was better than a stage comedy. Nothing could surpass the quaint peacock-like vanity of the girl mannequins who strutted up and down, moving their hips to accentuate the fall and flow of flounces...' (*The Bystander*, 27 July 1904), which challenged the eulogy that had been published in *The Smart Set* in May. Corelli was singularly unimpressed by the dinner gown entitled 'Red Mouth of a Venomous Flower', which she dismissed as 'a harmless-looking girl in a bright scarlet toilette' (a judgement possibly influenced by the fact that the name of the gown was a quotation from Algernon Charles Swinburne, of whom the strait-laced Corelli came to disapprove). In her *Couture Culture: A Study in Modern Art and Fashion* (2003), Nancy Troy makes pertinent comparisons between Lucile Ltd and the dynamics of Paul Poiret's presentation and marketing of fashion, as well as his preoccupation with Orientalism. Alistair O'Neill's *London – after a Fashion* (2007) includes a perceptive investigation of the Lucile phenomenon in terms of the house's reliance on theatricality and its heady, erotic brew of shimmering gowns, alluring mannequins and seductive ambiance.

Gowns and refined tailoring by Lucile have been included in a number of key fashion exhibitions, including 'Lady of Fashion. Heather Firbank and what she wore between 1908 and 1921' (V&A, 1960), Cecil Beaton's 'Fashion: An Anthology' (V&A 1971), 'Infra Apparel'

(The Costume Institute, Metropolitan Museum, 1993) and 'Cubism and Fashion' (The Costume Institute, Metropolitan Museum, 1998). In 2005 an exhibition of her work, 'Designing the It Girl: Lucile and Her Style', was organized by the graduate students (Fashion and Textile Studies: History, Theory, Museum Practice) at the Fashion Institute of Technology, New York; the show drew on the important Lucile collection in the FIT's Gladys Marcus Library Special Collections. In the same year Lucile featured in 'The London Look' (Museum of London). Edwardian dress has generally formed a brief starting point for surveys of twentieth-century fashion but only rarely has it been brought into sharp focus. Ann Coleman's scholarly *The Opulent Era: Fashions of Worth, Doucet and Pingat* (1989) is a notable exception and similarly catalogues such as *Style and Splendour* (Anne Kjellberg and Susan North, V&A 2005) scrupulously examine a selection of Edwardian couture – these texts point up the relatively poor survival rate of fragile, early 1900s afternoon and evening dress. With its mannered form and highly elaborate overlaid decoration, the style is perhaps not as accessible as, say, a 1920s shift dress, or the subject as immediate as post-war modernism.

This book's prime focus is the fashion album *From Lucile Ltd. Autumn 1905*. Although it precludes a tactile experience, the facsimile is the next best thing to the album itself. It presents *From Lucile Ltd. Autumn 1905* in its entirety – the designs can now be contemplated (without harm to the originals) much as they would have been scrutinized by potential clients over a hundred years ago. The V&A's skilled photographers have meticulously captured the intricate detail and colours of the original watercolours and fabrics. The album is interpreted in the context of clothes worn by, and the activities of, the *beau monde* four years after Edward VII had ascended the throne, when high society was at its sparkling zenith. At its heart was the Court, a showpiece for extravagant living and luxurious dress, providing some of Lucile's most influential clients. Many were delighted at royalty's endorsement of conspicuous consumption. *The Lady*, on 22 June 1905, gushed: 'Certainly we now have a brilliant court. The King and Queen do everything in the most magnificent style and I doubt if any court in Europe can compare with ours… .' It was just about this time that Lucile released her album of designs for Autumn 1905. It is a fascinating collection revealing fashion on the cusp – still rooted in the late nineteenth century but anticipating a redirection of style that took hold a couple of years later. It is seminal in Lucile's development, containing the seeds of her approach to fabrics, colour, decoration, cut and construction that she was to make her own and refine over the next 30 years.

Lucile also worked with words. Magazines and newspapers, from *Vogue* to *Weldon's Ladies' Journal*, came to regard her as a fashion guru and for some twenty years she provided lively columns pronouncing on a wide range of fashion-related topics. The extra income was welcome, as was the opportunity to publicize Lucile Ltd. Her comments are often eloquent as well as enlightening: describing the capricious nature of fashion, she wrote, in the *New York American Examiner* (1910), 'Fashion is such a whirling dervish, such a whirligig, fickle and changeable as a coquette.' She took every opportunity to promote her belief that dressmaking was an art and to pursue her crusade to make clothes that beautified women. Ever the romantic, her prose is littered with little fantasies such as '… and on her feet silver Cinderella slippers with buckles' (American *Good Housekeeping*, December 1912). On the other hand, she often conjured up cartoon-like images (again, in the *New York American Examiner*): 'Some of the corsets are awful and make the wearers look as if they have a veranda all around them.' In 1930 she declared that the back view of a young woman motorcyclist (riding pillion) resembled a frog (*Weldon's Ladies' Journal*, August 1930). She dealt with the sartorial needs of all varieties of women – plump, thin, plain or otherwise – but considered that artistic dress looked best on moody, slender types. Womanly allure, requiring a low, sweet voice, gentle manner and elegant movement, was a critical factor – in tandem with her 'gowns of emotion' it ensured success. Her journalism is amusing and informative (if often self-aggrandising), and reveals her complete dedication to fashion – she even dreamt new designs. Her columns contained practical instruction, but it is often her typically lyrical passages that gave her readers insight into how her designs worked. Most memorably, she wrote, in 1910: 'There is only one real fashion, and that is different with every woman. It is the outward draping of the soul, her individuality, her physical ensemble is the thing that interprets and harmonises with her'.[6]

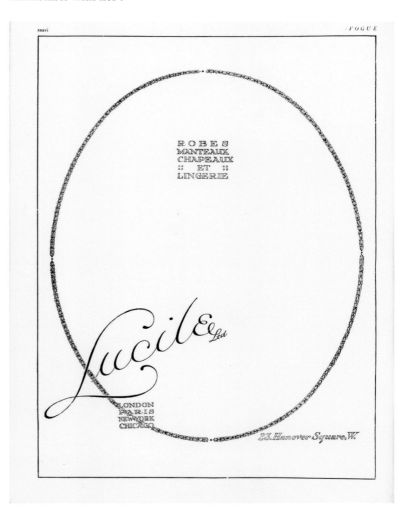

Chapter One '…Most bewitching gowns…' 1890s–1905

An Edwardian *élégante* required a range of 'sporty', tailored ensembles for travelling or sporting activities, as well as for country or seaside sojourns. Additionally, she needed ultra-fashionable 'tailor-mades', such as Lucile's 'An Episode', for town wear. In a rare occurrence, a watercolour for this chic *toilette de visite* (*see page 121*) matches an archive photograph of the actual costume (*opposite*, in reverse poses). These images reveal how scrupulously Lucile followed the design, with its oversize medallion fastenings, its short, body moulding basque and its long, flowing skirt. Her ruse of naming designs permitted her unusual licence, and 'An Episode' hints at a secret romantic assignation. Sharing beauty and an assertive air, the two mannequins, real and imagined, collude with Lucile's fantasy. Photographer Mabel Lomnitz captured the subtle sheen of soft wool against velvet revers and cuffs – a combination that was all the rage in 1905. Enhancing the photographic composition, an open *en tout cas* (which doubled as an umbrella or parasol) is balanced on one shoulder while a pale-coloured, tilted toque replaces the design's black, lace-bedecked bowler.

'…most bewitching gowns…'[1]

'When I commence a creation I study the form of the subject first and then the material and then the colour'.[2] Throughout her long career in fashion, Lucile remained true to these tenets, believing that long, graceful lines suited most women: she was arguably at her best composing svelte, trailing gowns redolent of pleasure and romance. She joined the ranks of London court dressmakers in 1895 as Mrs Lucy Wallace (her first married name), although she had been earning a living making clothes for a coterie of fashionable friends and acquaintances since the beginning of the decade. She overcame the then unladylike stigma of being 'in trade' and worked tirelessly to elevate her *métier*.

In the mid-1890s, the very time when Lucy Wallace was establishing her business, warnings had been sounded about ventures such as hers, which demanded energy, dedication and resourcefulness as well as capital and experience.[3] Lady dressmakers in pursuit of wealth or fame were cautioned that few would flourish and many would be undermined by the 'special' (low) prices expected by friends. Indeed, many years later, recollecting her money worries, Lucile would identify non-payment by rich friends as 'one of the most serious handicaps' a dressmaker had to face.[4] Yet, although she lacked a highly tuned financial sense, for many years her enterprise flourished: she had an abundance of drive, ambition and artistic talent, and steered her business from a modest family-based activity via increasingly prestigious addresses to Lucile Ltd, housed in the eighteenth-century splendour of 23 Hanover Square at a time when the Square was a beehive of chic dressmakers and milliners.

Elinor Glyn (1864–1943), destined to achieve fame and notoriety for her romantic novels, was Lucy's younger sister, and together they delighted in the pleasures of designing and making their own clothes. Lucy had excellent practical skills (first apparent in that familiar childhood pastime of making doll's dresses), was an original colourist and revealed a highly inventive touch. Giving the business a significant boost while acknowledging her sister's 'genius for making smart clothes',[5] in 1892 Elinor commissioned Lucy to design and make her wedding gown, bridesmaid's dresses and trousseau for her socially advantageous marriage to Clayton Glyn (a wealthy landowner and descendant of Sir Richard Carl Glyn, Lord Mayor of London). Years later, Lucy could not recall the child bridesmaids' outfits (apart from their touches of yellow, which apparently caused a lot of comment), but with typical aplomb recollected that Elinor resembled 'the living incarnation of a fairy-tale princess'.[6]

Revealing her informed interest in fashion, Elinor, a clever artist, created an illustrated record comprising annotated ink sketches, depicting over a hundred gowns worn by herself and her sister between 1890 and 1897. Lucy had designed, made and remodelled many of the outfits. Elinor drew ensembles from her trousseau as well as her 1892 wedding dress (*opposite, left*). Describing the heavy white satin gown with its pronounced gigot sleeves, Elinor indicated Lucy's nascent unconventional approach to structure in the 'stretched' bodice 'fastening under arm no seams [*sic*]'[7] (in the 1890s a bodice was invariably fastened along the centre front or back). Elinor's incisive line drawings indicate the complexities of a fashionable wardrobe at that time, and her succinct commentaries highlight such features as a skirt so full that it needed 12 yards of pale rose-pink muslin and bouffant sleeves, each one tightly packed with 12 yards of frilled, satin-edged chiffon. She illustrated how a gown could be reworked to extend its life: her wedding ensemble was transformed twice for evening wear while other toilettes kept their skirts but received new bodices or fresh trimmings. Elinor also documented fantasy attire of the type that was later to become central to the Lucile operation – costume for theatricals (initially amateur) and fancy dress for balls or *tableaux*. A lavish Mary, Queen of Scots ensemble (dated January 1893) was commissioned by Elinor for a *tableau vivant* at Shipley Hall, Derbyshire. Costumed by Lucy,

ABOVE Full-length photograph of Elinor Glyn. Tightly corseted, Elinor perches on the arm of a chair with hand on hip to emphasize her curvaceous form. Over a lace camisole, she wears a low-necked, Charmeuse and tulle gown (bodice and skirt) with an open-fronted lace overdress and flounced petticoat bound in satin to match rouleaux around the neck. Elinor patronized Paris designers (including Doucet) but frequently wore designs by her sister. It is possible that this delicate creation, involving ribbon rosettes and tiny fabric flowers, was by Lucile. H. Walter Barnet, 1903.

an 1895 performance of French playwright Victorien Sardou's melodrama *Diplomacy*, given by the dashing (but almost bankrupt) Lord Rosslyn at Dysart House in Fife, had Elinor playing the character of Dora in a white china silk tea gown fastened with jewelled dragons and day gown in bright cerise with white and yellow trimmings (*above, right*). Able to manipulate modest fabrics as well as sumptuous silks and embroideries, in an optically dramatic cotton gown for summer 1895 Lucy used the stripes to enhance a tiny waist and emphasize the pouched bodice and enormous gigot sleeves (*overleaf, top*). The highlight of 1897, the year of Queen Victoria's Diamond Jubilee, was the Duchess of Devonshire's fancy-dress ball. The *crème de la crème* assiduously researched their costumes before calling upon their designers and dressmakers. For this much-photographed and widely published extravaganza *les grands couturiers*, such as Worth and Paquin, provided expensively ornate costumes of supreme magnificence. Lucy transformed the society hostess Mrs Willie James into the Archduchess Elizabeth (*overleaf, centre*) in 'a costume of stiff silver tissue, through which glimmered an underdress of antique cerise taffeta. The reproduction was quite a chef d'oeuvre; the long pointed corsage being enhanced by priceless point lace entwined with roses in palest pink; those flowers, in various sizes, were scattered over the entire toilette and gave to it a charming pre-Raphaelite effect.'[8]

With her green eyes and the Sutherland family vivid-red hair set against a porcelain-white complexion, Elinor possessed a strikingly elegant presence and wore clothes with enviable panache. In the 1890s, moving in the upper echelons of society, she proved the ideal ambassadress for Lucy's fashions – admirers of her style made their way to her sister's dressmaking establishment. Writing retrospectively in 1921, Lady Angela Forbes was

LEFT Pen-and-ink sketch of wedding gown, Mrs Lucy Wallace for Elinor Glyn on her marriage to Clayton Louis Glyn, 27 April 1892, St George's, Hanover Square. Elinor declared that her sister had surpassed herself with this white satin dress. Fichu, veil and sleeves were of antique Honiton lace. The brocade train, like the skirt, was edged with ruched satin. Accessories included a diamond tiara (a present from the groom to his 'fairy Queen'), brooches, a cross and strings of pearls, while gardenias, stephanotis and orange blossom formed the bouquet.

RIGHT Pen-and-ink sketch of theatrical costume by Mrs Lucy Wallace for Elinor Glyn in an amateur performance of *Diplomacy* in 1895. Such enormous bouffant sleeves were typical of the period – sometimes they were kept 'inflated' by tulle frills or, most extraordinarily, by light, flexible frames made of feather bone.

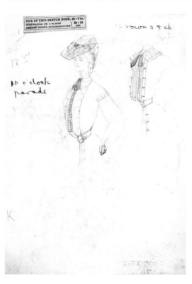

very grateful to Elinor 'because she gave me the address of her sister Mrs Wallace –"Lucille" [*sic*] of to-day's fame', adding: 'She made the most lovely frocks for £8!!'[9] In February 1894 *The Queen* heralded Lucy Wallace as 'the presiding genius of the Maison Lucile', making note of 'the lovely lingerie, the silken petticoats, and Parisian corsets, which are strewn in endless variety about the beautifully decorated rooms of the Maison Lucile'. A few months later this magazine noted that although the Maison Lucile was in its infancy it had 'gained the pleasing reputation of being one of the smartest houses in London, and is largely patronised by women who are past mistresses in the art of dress'.[10]

Lucy Wallace's enterprise was flourishing in a difficult market. In London alone, competition was fierce on many levels. For those who could not afford the bespoke services of a private dressmaker, there were many ways to stretch a dress allowance. In addition to the might of the big retail stores with their well-stocked costume departments, there were countless smaller ready-to-wear outlets. Many large shops ran highly efficient mail order departments to meet the increasingly popular habit of shopping by post. Home-dressmaking was a low-budget option, nurtured by paper patterns of the latest modes and an abundance of fabrics and haberdashery, as well as plentiful advice in women's magazines. The wealthy had personal maids – skilled needle-women who cleaned, repaired and remodelled their expensive clothes. At the turn of the century Mrs Lucy Wallace was among more than 2,000 private dressmakers in Central London; of these, some 400 were listed as court dressmakers (indicating that they were versed in the protocol and dress code for presentations and other royal occasions).[11] In this densely populated profession, up to 50 businesses collapsed each year. But Lucy Wallace shrewdly established a niche for the Lucile 'look', and in a few years it became a leading concern alongside eminent Edwardian costumiers such as Reville and Rossiter, Redfern and Mascotte.

In 1900 she married again and became Lady Duff Gordon. Cosmo Duff Gordon (1862–1931) was a Scot, who, in 1896, had become the 5th Baronet Duff – his occupation was described (on Lucile company papers) as 'Baronet'. He was handsome (with an imposing moustache), six feet tall, and athletic – considered one of the best épée swordsmen in the country. He was part of Lord Desborough's British fencing team that won a silver medal in the 1906 interim Olympic Games, Athens, and he served on the fencing organizing committee for London's Olympic Games in 1908. Inevitably his title added a certain cachet to Lucile's activities. It did the business no harm, either, when Maud Cassel came to Lucile for the gown in which she married Wilfred Ashley in 1901. Highly strung, amusing but of precariously delicate health, Maud was the only daughter of the enormously wealthy and influential financier, Sir Ernest Cassel, adviser and friend to Edward, Prince of Wales, who attended the wedding with his powerful, affluent and distinguished 'set' (including his mistress, Mrs Keppel). Maud's gown of soft white satin was a lyrical Lucile composition involving pleated chiffon, flounced antique lace, flower sprays, cross-laced silver ribbons with diamond buttons and an elaborate cloth-of-silver train.

Heralding the approach of the 1902 Season, it was noted in *The Queen* (12 April) that the Maison Lucile was 'synonymous with good style'. The readership was assured that they would find clothes that were 'most original and suitable to all the different occasions of a season'. Perhaps for the first time a journalist makes mention of Lucile's picturesque technique of giving her gowns 'gracious names' evocative of their colour, purpose, composition or associations (usually romantic). Her sense of the dramatic was offended 'that some creation of mine, the expression of a mood, should be spoken of only as "number nine"… So I gave them all names and personalities of their own.'[12] The press and audiences were fascinated and amused by these names, which gave Lucile gowns added appeal and

TOP Striped gown, illustrated at the opening of the Royal Academy's Summer Exhibition in *The Queen*, May 1895. No doubt Mrs Wallace was delighted that a full page was devoted to her work, which was described as 'A cotton frock from the Maison Lucile, 24, Old Burlington Street. Black and white stripe cotton, trimmed at the neck and wrists with either black or coloured ribbon, over which are turned little finely tucked muslin and lace points.'

CENTRE Mrs Willie James (considered to be one of the smartest of the Smart Set) in fancy dress as the Archduchess Elizabeth at the Devonshire House Ball, 2 July 1897. Maison Lucile supplied the costume. Mrs Willie James (d. 1929) was a beauty, socialite, philanthropist, talented amateur actress and mother of Edward James (poet and patron of the Surrealists). With her American husband she entertained lavishly (especially during the Goodwood races) at West Dean Park near Chichester, Sussex, and was one of Edward VII's favourites. Lucile was grateful to her for introducing royal clients and was inordinately proud to have Victoria Eugenie ('Ena'), Queen of Spain (1887–1969), Marie, Queen of Romania (1875–1938) and the Duchess of York (later Queen Mary, 1867–1953) among her regal customers. Lafayette Archive, V&A

BOTTOM 'Ten O'Clock Parade' preliminary, annotated pencil sketch for a day gown (bodice and skirt) for the private view of 'Costume Suggestions', 28 April 1904 and/or the musical play, *Catch of the Season* (which included a Church Parade sequence). Lucile had an increasingly busy schedule, so her initial ideas were hurriedly drawn and usually unfinished. Some notes were made as she sketched while others were added later in haste, sometimes by her staff – the spelling is not always accurate and information is not consistent from one outfit to the next. This brown, neatly tailored gown cost 12 guineas and two versions of the bodice are shown. Sketchbook, 1904

made excellent copy – for instance, it was reported in *The Smart Set*, in May 1904, 'I saw the cruel red lips, white teeth, and shining eyes of the beauty who would wear the dress called "The Vampire".' Lucile explained that she had occasional help in the quest for suitably resonant titles, which were invented or culled from a wide range of sources: 'The Tender Grace of a Day that is Dead' (*see page 65*) came from Alfred, Lord Tennyson's poignant 'Break, Break, Break' (*Poems*, 1842), while 'Red Mouth of a Venomous Flower' (a dinner gown) was adapted from Algernon Swinburne's Sadian poem 'Dolores' (*Poems and Ballads*, 1866). 'Ten O'Clock Parade' (1902) made reference to the Church Parade, Society's custom of strolling in Hyde Park on Sundays, and was a smart morning gown in pale, almost shrimp, pink tweed; this notion was repeated two years later, in April 1904, at Lucile Ltd's private view, 'Costume Suggestions Being Studies in the Expression of Personality in Curves and Colours'. One of Lucile's innovative fashion parades, it was covered by *The Smart Set*, who lavishly praised Lucile as 'a gifted woman who has amplified and perfected the art of beautiful attire until it has become in her hands a thing of awe… an apostle of the cult of curves, the religion of beauty' and 'an artist who is at once a poet and high priest of the beautiful'. *The Smart Set*'s 'About Town' society and fashion columnist was clearly besotted with the distinctive focus and the subtle magnetism of Lucile's fashion parades (which continued throughout summer) and published two further glowing reports in June and July. These explored Lucile as a 'psychologist in dress' and as 'the high priestess of a cult'. In that charmed place, her 'Temple of Dress', the reporter took note of the delicate grey-tinted programmes, the scented silk petals of 3,000 hand-made roses, and audience reaction that shifted from 'critical intelligence' via 'pleased surprise' to conclude in 'supreme rapture'.

The on-stage procession was themed around a socialite's day and Society events beginning with 'Morning Confidences' (*left*) and 'Ready For The Ten O'Clock in Hyde Park'. The Sunday morning Church Parade in the park was a feast of Edwardian conspicuous consumption: the very latest fashions were on view and its purpose was to look and be looked at. The press dedicated many columns to meticulous descriptions of these Sunday gowns and their elegant owners. In similar detail they documented the Season's events, and who wore what and where. Symbiotically, the London Season that dominated the activities of the Edwardian upper classes offered journalists a structure and a rhythm just as its sartorial demands provided dressmakers (including Lucile) with an affluent clientele.

Lucile's 1905 album is a cornucopia of designs, fabrics and trimmings, and over the course of more than 100 years it has acquired a multiplicity of meanings.[13] At face value the designs represent ultra-fashionable clothes showing the last vestiges of nineteenth-century style that could be made to order for women belonging to an Edwardian elite – Society's 'finest'. In the 1890s the 9th Duke of Marlborough held this to be some 200 families of rank. *The Queen* nominated this clique 'The Upper Ten Thousand', publishing meticulous lists of its activities at home and abroad. Most poetically Elinor Glyn pictured it as 'the fairy ring within which danced a circle of families entitled to enjoy its privileges on account of birth and tradition'.[14] The album *From Lucile Ltd. Autumn 1905* illuminates a peak of early 1900s extravagance and marks a high point in Lucile's enterprise, now established in 23 Hanover Square: the 'embodiment of all my dreams'.[15] Contained within the 69 watercolours are elements that became permanent fixtures in the Lucile repertoire and, though not unique to the label, were henceforward indissolubly linked with the name. Fabric snips are juxtaposed in Fauve-like, powerful and sometimes clashing colour combinations, involving bright oranges, pinks, purples and blues, prefiguring the feast of colours that astounded audiences at the Paris

ABOVE 'Morning Confidences', the first 'Suggestion' from the private view of 'Costume Suggestions', 28 April 1904. A rare photograph of *déshabillé* by Lucile showing the mannequin in a diaphanous *saut de lit* daringly open to reveal a princess-line 'combination' of boned satin 'corsage' and lace-trimmed petticoat and fragile beribboned camisole. Line drawings and photographs of corsets and lingerie were commonplace in the Edwardian fashion press but it was most unusual for undress to be featured on a 'living model' by a designer in this semi-public manner. 'The New Art of Woman', *The Smart Set*, May 1904

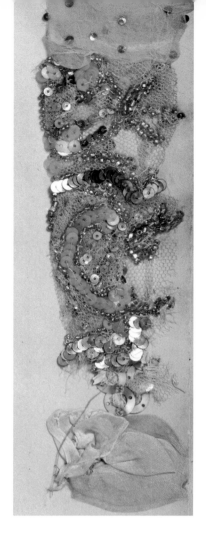

BELOW:

TOP 'L'Allegro' evening gown
(*see page 159*) *From Lucile Ltd. Autumn
1905*

BOTTOM 'L'Allegro' detail of samples:
two bright pink satin fragments, and a
floral motif embroidered in flat metallic
strip (plain and embossed) in pink and
gold gilt.

launch of the Ballets Russes in 1909. At the other end of the spectrum are gentle harmonies in pastel hydrangea and sweet pea shades which, in conjunction with fluid layers of laces, chiffons and embroideries, became a Lucile hallmark. The album gives a unique insight into the extraordinary range and quality of textiles and garnitures available at that time.

Lucile subscribed to the Edwardian passion for lace, using it liberally for complete garments as well as collars, sleeves, jabots, rabats and every conceivable edging. Fashion historian and V&A curator James Laver, in his *Age of Extravagance* (1955), marvelled at the 'veritable mania for lace. …there was hardly any part of a woman's dress which was not adorned with this most expensive form of decoration'. Perhaps for financial reasons, Lucile tended to avoid costly hand-made lace, preferring to layer machine lace within confections of chiffon frills, silk rosebuds and bébé ribbons so skilfully that it hardly mattered that it was not 'real'. Lace snobbism abounded: in *The Visits of Elizabeth* Elinor Glyn described a petticoat with 'common lace on it', a criticism that could not be levelled at her sister's exquisite compositions. According to society and fashion columnists, beauties moved in 'clouds' of lace, chiffon and tulle, and fashion guru Mrs Eric Pritchard instructed readers that 'Fashion decrees that lace shall be worn in every form' (*The Lady's Realm*, 1901).

Artificial flowers bedecked fashionable clothes and accessories (particularly hats), whatever the season. Such was the demand for the finest replicas that flower-makers in Paris had to complete a three- to five-year apprenticeship. It was considered the height of chic to combine hand-crafted with real flowers. Lucile was entranced with the prettiness and femininity of rococo dress: its flowered silks, ribbon *échelles*, artificial flowers and delicate flounces, as well as its 'eroticism and succulence which can best be seen in portraits by Boucher in the 1740s'.[16] Silk florets, especially pale pink rosebuds, were dear to both Lucile and Elinor – 'one wore negligees of lovely satins with little mule slippers which had posies of Lucile silk roses as buckles to match the trimmings. They were feminine and alluring.'[17] It seems that Elinor laboured painstakingly over the hundreds of silk roses that adorned her own boudoir. In the 1905 collection, tiny silk rosebuds on green silk rouleau stems circle around necklines, sleeves and hems, or nestle under flounces of frail *mousseline de soie*. The Hanover Square salon boasted a seductive room of 'Roses and Reveries', which lulled clients into the right mood to choose *lingerie de luxe*.

By 1905 Lucile's role in the rituals of the Season was well established. In tune with the aspirations of young débutantes (and their mothers), Lucile attired them in gorgeous presentation gowns, then provided an array of dresses, costumes and lingerie for the subsequent dances, balls, dinners, luncheons, picnics, garden parties, race meetings, and town and country-house visits (a sequence so amusingly captured in Elinor's novel, *The Visits of Elizabeth*). To satisfy demand, Lucile eventually opened a débutante department (as had a number of Paris designers before her). Designs for *jeunes filles* were endowed with a carefully calculated degree of seductive appeal – the aim was to secure a suitable marriage contract, preferably before the year was out and, as Lady Rothschild declared, 'for a really successful maiden hardly ever going unmarried through more than three seasons'.[18] At least ten gowns, designed with young women in mind, are included in the album, bearing names such as 'When Life's Young Pleasure's Woo' and 'The Elusive Joy of Youth'; further to evoke virginal innocence, the prevailing colours are white, pale lilac, baby blues and pinks. A bride-to-be was assured of a luscious wedding gown and trousseau from 23 Hanover Square. The Lucile trousseau designed for Queen Victoria's granddaughter, Princess Margaret, 'Daisy', of Connaught, reflected H.R.H.'s fondness for pale pink and blue and, prior to her marriage (in June 1905, to Prince Gustav Adolph of Sweden), the trousseau was displayed for a chosen few in Clarence House. Luxury silks from

ABOVE Two details of pastel-coloured samples: sequinned tulle and silk chiffon. Silks, embroidered silver gilt floral motif and lace. *From Lucile Ltd. Autumn 1904*

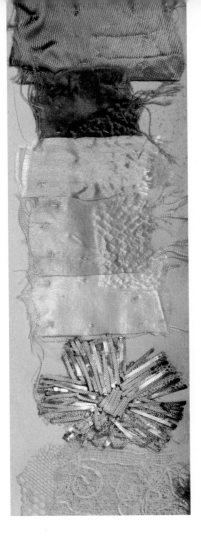

Lyons and the finest trimmings were specially purchased for this important commission. An impressive collection, it featured a typical Lucile profusion of embroideries, chiffons and silks – 'recognizable by her finishing touches… of minute buttons, and little frills of lace and ribbon'.[19] Among the works singled out for description was a tea gown of 'special beauty… of "maiden's blush" rose satin, very soft indeed'.[20] Lucile's profits grew and the workforce expanded as the client base increased – the needs of débutantes and brides were satisfied, as were those of married customers (many with husbands of wealth and standing) – their stylish appearance was assured in Lucile outfits with a sophisticated gloss.

Lucile's and Elinor's autobiographies identify key Lucile Ltd clients and hint at others; more have come to light and many remain to be discovered. That excellent sales tool, the grapevine, spread the word about Lucile. In the quest for new looks at reasonable cost (Lucile clothes were not over-priced),[21] women known for their chic found their way to 23 Hanover Square. In poetic vein she made much of her empathy with customers and the consequent 'gowns of emotion' created to fit the personality of each client. Like her fashion parades, troupe of mannequins and seductive interiors, this was an undeniably brilliant ploy. However, it was standard practice for a designer to study a customer and create garments that enhanced their individuality. In November 1896 Marie A. Belloc interviewed Jean-Philippe Worth (artistic director of the great couture house Maison Worth founded by his father, Charles Frederick) for *The Lady's Realm*. He noted: 'My father was among the first to dress his clients with a view to their natural peculiarities, colouring etc.' Another such designer was Madame Régy of Portman Square, who was described in *The Woman at Home* (February 1898) as 'one of those artistic dressmakers who are a boon to femininity. With unerring tact and taste she studies the individuality of her customers, suiting their requirements and dressing them to the best advantage.' Lucile elevated this process to new heights. She gathered many fascinating and beautiful customers, some who ran with the Smart Set (derided for its 'vanity, extravagance and lack of high principle' by a sanctimonious Marie Corelli),[22] famous actresses, some impeccable members of the aristocracy, and royalty. Among the 'professional beauties' and society hostesses Lucile dressed were Frances Evelyn, 'Daisy', Countess of Warwick (*page 26, top*), Georgina, Countess of Dudley, Violet, Duchess of Rutland and Lady Angela Forbes (*page 26, centre*), whose images (sometimes wearing Lucile) regularly graced the society pages.

Lucile's work also attracted the strong-minded, none more so than Margot Asquith, wife of the Prime Minister, who was acknowledged to be a sort of whirlwind in petticoats and stirred up a national furore when she invited Paul Poiret to show his collection at 10 Downing Street in 1909. Another woman of firm opinions, the American-born socialite and actress Mrs Cora Brown Potter patronized Lucile for dramatic gowns in colours that emphasized her flaming red hair (*see page 28*). Lily Elsie (*page 26, bottom*) was one of the most famous and most photographed pre-war stage celebrities who wore Lucile's designs. Lucile also listed 'the beautiful Mrs Atherton' among her customers, adding a sympathetic picture of her tragic life: in 1911 the litigious Mabel Louisa Atherton was involved in a slander case; she sued a motorist for knocking her down in a dress worth 18 guineas in 1917, and finally in 1919, after a family scandal, she committed suicide using a shot-gun while arrayed in evening gown and pearls. In gentler mode, Heather Firbank (sister of the novelist Ronald Firbank), who 'had beauty and adorned it with exquisite clothes of a heather colour to complement her name',[23] went to Lucile for gowns in her favourite spectrum, pale mauve to imperial purple.

Towards the end of April Society began to drift back to London for the beginning of the Season in May. This gave time for up-to-the-minute

BELOW:

TOP Detail of bodice, 'The Tender Grace of a Day that is Dead'. Lucile perfected the technique of scattering diminutive pink silk rosebuds on a pale foundation over which she floated delicate, semi-transparent chiffon or voile. Here tiny buds can be glimpsed through the layer of mid-green chiffon.

BOTTOM Detail of page 89 showing a typical Lucile rosebud in silk gauze in two shades of pink and pale green.

OVERLEAF Fabrics and trimmings for five ensembles (left to right, see pages 77, 131, 107, 90, 149, 77)

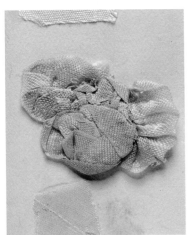

BEAUTIFUL WOMEN IN THE SOCIAL WORLD

LADY ANGELA FORBES

11545 © ROTARY PHOTO. E.C.   MISS LILY ELSIE.   FOULSHAM & BANFIELD.

modes to be studied in fashion magazines, for last season's clothes to be remodelled accordingly and for new ensembles to be purchased in London and Paris. Memoirs of Edwardian aristocratic and professional beauties indicate that Paris haute couture, especially the houses of Worth, Laferrière, Redfern, Paquin and Doucet, were favoured for occasional, high-profile creations such as a ball gown, wedding gown or parts of one's trousseau, while London dressmakers completed the wardrobe – unless, like Consuelo, Duchess of Marlborough (daughter of the American multi-millionaire William Vanderbilt), one was extraordinarily rich. Like most of her successful London competitors (such as Mrs Mason and Kate Reily)[24] Lucile had to cope with huge demand before fashionable occasions including presentations at Court, first nights at Covent Garden, Ascot, Glorious Goodwood and Cowes.

By late July, the Season was over and 'the very flower and pinnacle of the London world'[25] left town, embarking on country-house visits or travelling to watering-places abroad. The time was approaching to attend to one's winter clothes, or, as *The Lady's Realm* put it (October 1900), 'commence the general harassing and worrying of our tailors and dressmakers'. *From Lucile Ltd. Autumn 1905* illustrates the range of attire that a well-dressed woman could ponder (for a fee of 20 guineas – a guinea was a pound and a shilling) in personal consultation with Lucile.[26] The designs split obligingly into day and evening wear, then subdivide into numerous, frequently interchangeable, categories. Fine distinctions between a walking costume, travelling ensemble, promenade costume and a *toilette de visite* are not easy to discern. Like the fabrics of fashion, the language of fashion was rich, sometimes bewildering, and littered with French terms. Paris remained fashion's fountainhead and it was considered chic to use French nomenclature – businesses (including Lucile) added Maison or Madame to their names, seeking to promote their image and attract clients.

Each tiny 1905 watercolour mannequin conforms to the popular sinuous shape: the torso thrust forward, the posterior projected back and the waist nipped in. This substructure was engineered by corsets over which slid layers of filmy lingerie. Constance Peel asserted that Lucile introduced 'a new make of stay which kept the figure flat in front and emphasised its size below the waist at the back'.[27] In her autobiography Lucile overplayed her role in the transition from substantial underwear to gossamer lingerie – she was definitely not alone in this revolution but deservedly won a reputation for underclothing 'as delicate as cobwebs'.[28] For cold weather, the album features soft woollen tweeds and a desirable but costly supple broadcloth known as faced cloth, face-cloth or simply cloth with a slight nap and subtle sheen. During the early 1900s a costume consisted of bodice or coat, plus matching skirt. Attention focused on the upper garments: in addition to colour, it was lavish, ingenuous ornamentation and subtleties of cut that distinguished one from another. Novel sleeves were also of enormous importance, and Lucile excelled in their complexities. So crucial was an interesting sleeve that magazines featured intriguing illustrations of amputated arms dressed in 'new' sleeves – elaborate variations on a theme. Composed of many yards of fabric, skirts often had easily removable decoration to simplify remodelling. Almost all the 1905 day wear is worn over blouses with tall, stand-up or stock collars that compelled wearers to hold their head up high; such collars were kept upright with supports of steel, feather or whale bone. The agony of a constricting corset was matched by the pain of these stiffeners – the Duchess of Sermoneta tells of them rubbing 'little wounds all round one's neck'.[29]

For a country-house 'Saturday to Monday', clothes to cover every eventuality would be packed into huge, often domed trunks. Some women reluctantly endured shooting parties, dragging their tailor-mades (some by Lucile) through the mud. Though walking skirts usually lacked

TOP Portrait of Frances Evelyn, 'Daisy', Countess of Warwick, in the 1890s. Lady Warwick (1861–1938), renowned for her beauty, fascinating personality and exquisite taste in dress, had an intimate liaison with the Prince of Wales that lasted nearly a decade. She entertained extravagantly at Warwick Castle and Easton Lodge Estate, and in the mid-1890s she became increasingly involved with charitable projects and socialism. Elinor Glyn introduced her to Lucile and in turn she passed the contact around her prestigious circle of friends and family. Mrs Eric Pritchard dedicated *The Cult of Chiffon* (1902) to 'The Countess of Warwick, to her who makes fashion beautiful and "the beautiful" the fashion'. Elinor thought of her as 'the sun's rays', stating that 'Hers was that supreme personal charm which I later described as "It", because it is quite indefinable and does not depend on beauty or wit, although she possessed both in the highest degree.' (*Romantic Adventure*, 1936)

CENTRE Portrait of Lady Angela Forbes (1876–1950), c.1910. In the early 1890s on a visit to Easton Lodge (the Essex country house belonging to her half-sister, the Countess of Warwick) she met Elinor Glyn who introduced her to Lucile gowns. Lucile's 'artistic' creations suited the lovely, young and vivacious Lady Angela Forbes, who was a daring horsewoman and something of an *enfant terrible*. In *Memories and Base Details* (1922) she reminisced about Lucile's 'wonderful collection of old collars which she used to adapt, and she gave me a lovely one which she put on my going away coat!' *Everywoman's Encyclopaedia*, 'Beautiful Women in the Social World', 1911

BOTTOM Postcard of Lily Elsie (1886–1962), c.1910. Seated on a table, the actress, described as 'drenchingly lovely' by Cecil Beaton, in his *Book of Beauty*, wears a demure summer day ensemble by Lucile. The prim voile blouse has tiny pin tucks and lace-edged collar, while rows of large covered buttons (a favourite Lucile trimming) decorate the skirt's front and side kick pleat. A large picture hat (in *Merry Widow* vein) adds drama to the outfit. Foulsham and Banfield, published by Rotary Photographic co.

trains and had hems a few inches above ground they were still long and got filthy. Almost all skirts in the album are trained; they look graceful, artfully draped along the ground, but in reality they swept over grimy streets and floors, 'their only use consisting in much reducing the labours of the crossing-sweepers'.[30] In spite of countless skirt-lifter inventions, women usually hoisted them with one hand. Etiquette decreed that during this process, the arm should be kept close to the body and it was considered unladylike to stick the elbow out. The medical profession protested against trailing dresses as 'contrary to the rules of hygiene and cleanliness', explaining the dangers when they 'transfer noxious organisms'.[31] Of course muddy skirts made stalking or shooting even more of an ordeal for many country-house guests. Lady Cynthia Asquith, the Prime Minister's daughter-in-law, complained: 'I have to stand around for hours and hours in sodden woods watching gloomy men kill happy birds,'[32] and the unconventional beauty and socialite Lady Angela Forbes declared: 'I think crawling on one's tummy through bog and heather… is not the happiest way of spending a day.'[33] However, chill and miseries were banished by 'the five o'clock', when ladies stepped out of their muddy tweeds or riding habits and assembled for tea resplendent in their tea gowns. Lucile was renowned for exquisite tea gowns, but a pink peignoir (*see page 152*) is the nearest garment in the album to a tea gown. Lucile maintained that her success was founded upon an accordion-pleated tea gown commissioned by the MP's wife, the Hon. Mrs Arthur Brand (for a house party). Associated with romance and coquetry, the 'temptatious tea gown'[34] was much scrutinized by fashion journalists and featured in countless Edwardian chronicles. As a garment of 'illusion, poetry and mystic grace',[35] it was a perfect vehicle for Lucile's fantasies. After tea, with the help of a personal maid, the chore of clambering in and out of clothes was not ended: guests had to transform themselves once more for dining and evening entertainments.

Autumn 1905 portrays the gamut of evening attire from magnificent ball gowns complete with tiaras and perilously low décolletages to more demure dinner ensembles with slightly higher necklines and elaborate sleeves. Long white kid gloves and jewellery were *de rigueur*. Pearls, as were displayed on many of Lucile's diminutive mannequins, were Edwardian favourites. Queen Alexandra bedecked herself with pearls; Daisy, Princess of Pless (daughter of the Irish beauty and one-time mistress of the Prince of Wales, Mary 'Patsy' Cornwallis-West) was proud of 'the world famous rope of Pless pearls seven yards long';[36] and the diminutive Duchess of Marlborough appeared in 'cascades of pearls'.[37] Not all great houses were fully equipped with electric light (Queen Alexandra disliked its harshness), so evening dress was frequently seen by the soft glow of gas jets or more flatteringly by flickering candlelight. To maximize the sparkling impact of her creations Lucile scattered gowns with light-catching sequins, metallic silver and gold lace and coloured metal embroidery, these being in addition to the usual embellishments of lace edgings, chiffon ruches, bébé ribbons, silk flowers, tassels, pendants and minute shining tags.

LEFT Detail of woollen cloth bodice showing intricate decorative details involving silver soutache and matching buttons and passementerie devices. Tiny metallic buttons, beads or studs highlight the curved front panel, sleeve head and skirt pleats – known as 'nails' in the trade, they sparkled in the light were much used to enliven day wear. Lucile Ltd, 1905

OPPOSITE Bright green embroidered cloak over a gown for the American actress Mrs Cora Brown Potter (1857–1936) – probably for a recital. Like her sister, Lucile was always conscious of her red hair (then not considered *à la mode*); it undoubtedly promoted her sensitivity to colour and she knew what colours were best for her red-haired clients.

'Cora Potter with her piquant face and her mane of red hair which in moments of emotion came undone and poured over her like a magnificent mantle.'

After All, Elsie de Wolfe, 1935

'Her oval face, luxuriant auburn hair, intelligent and lively expression and clear cut features, distinguished her even in an age which was remarkable for feminine beauty.'

Mrs Brown Potter's obituary, The Times, 13 February 1936

In 1937, diarist and author Harold Nicolson (husband of Vita Sackville-West), looked back on 'The Edwardian Weekend'. He asked: 'Who among us to-day would really dress for church and dress for luncheon and dress for tea and dress again for dinner?'[38] Lucile catered for the last generation of women who did just that. Years later, she too observed (in her autobiography): 'Very few women would bother now to change their dresses five or six times a day, yet every Edwardian, with any claims to being well dressed, did so as a matter of course'.[39] The album is a multi-coloured litany of clothes which an elegant and privileged clientele could flaunt as the chill of winter descended in the year 1905. Above all, it tells of a period when women compelled their bodies into outlandish serpentine curves and had the leisure to consider every minutia of their wardrobe as etiquette demanded.

BELOW Detail of the evening gown 'Faute des Roses', revealing the complexities of a frilled chemisette and sleeve arrangement. The watercolour captures static perfection but in reality to get everything in the right place and properly adjusted the assistance of a lady's maid was essential. In Vita Sackville-West's *The Edwardians* (1930), the maid Button gathers up a 'lovely mass of taffeta and tulle' and holds the bodice open for the Duchess of Chevron to dive 'into the billows of her dress', then Button fastens a line of innumerable hooks up the back.

Chapter Two From Lucile Ltd. Autumn 1905
The Making, Meaning and Biography of the Album
The Facsimile
'Carresaute', an Evening Gown

The Autumn 1905 collection was presented in a sturdy ledger book of dark red American cloth over board.

The album was purchased from John Stait, account book manufacturer, whose shop was situated in Oxford Street, near to Hanover Square. The label is glued to the inside front cover.

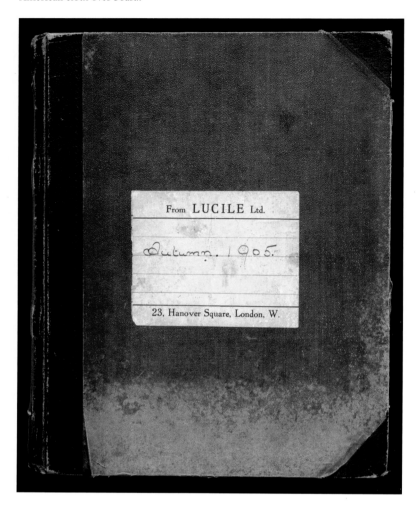

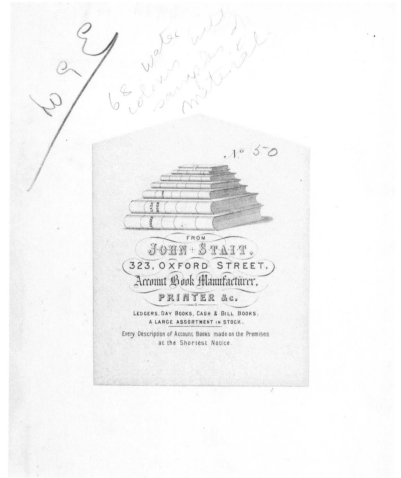

The Making, Meaning and Biography of From Lucile Ltd. Autumn 1905

Today, as in 1905, fashion houses compile seasonal albums with images of ensembles for the forthcoming collection, accompanied by fabric samples. Colour must be discerned in different lights, texture evaluated by touch: they cannot be successfully experienced or assessed electronically. The fashion album provides a compact and portable overview of a collection and serves as an interface between creator and consumer. Its role is to entice clients to place orders and, as such, it is central to the successful operation of a business. This essay explores the making of *From Lucile Ltd. Autumn 1905*, its shifting functions and its biography to the present day.

Once the styling and fabrication of Lucile's Autumn 1905 collection was finalized, and sample garments approved, work would have started on the album. The processes involved in transforming a sturdy ledger book into an appealing fashion album were considered, multi-skilled, labour-intensive and costly. An interesting comparison can be made here between the creation of such an artefact and a photograph album. In her study of photograph albums, photography historian Elizabeth Edwards has highlighted the presentational role of a photograph album as central to its function as a socially salient object.[1] For Lucile's album it was the combining, attaching and embedding of the various components – painted plates, fabrics and ledger book – that made it a functioning document.

One of the earliest stages would have been establishing the sequence of designs: the first page – a pale blue walking ensemble – would have been most carefully selected as it formed the prospective client's first impression. A member of Lucile's workroom staff, probably a junior 'hand', would have gathered together snippets of the fabrics and trimmings used for each ensemble and glued them carefully onto each page. (This is in contrast to

Letter of application written by 'Doré Madge' for the position of fashion artist at Lucile Ltd, 1912

the Autumn 1904 album, in which the fabrics are crudely hand-stitched into the pages.) Some fabrics are partially concealed, which suggests that the painted designs were applied subsequently.

The watercolour plates were painted by an accomplished but unnamed fashion artist (this was not uncommon). By 1905 fashion drawing was a recognized and relatively well-paid profession for young women (once married, few worked outside of the home). The main sources of employment were either a design studio, which undertook work for various clients, or a fashion retail environment. There is no evidence as to whether the fashion artist who painted these images worked in-house for Lucile Ltd or not. However, archival evidence does reveal that by 1912 Lucile did engage in-house fashion artists. A file contains four hand-written applications, accompanied by specimens of work, from young women in response to a job advertisement placed by the company in the *Daily Telegraph* on 4 December 1912 (*above*). Of all the hundreds of employees Lucile appointed over the years, it is remarkable that ephemeral documents were preserved to record these few applicants for posterity. Unfortunately, nothing survives to indicate which artist Lucile selected.

The fashion artist's skills, remit and profile were distinct from those of a fashion illustrator. An illustrator tended to create more impressionistic designs and present drawings as signed, finished artworks that could be effectively reproduced and disseminated in print. Irrespective of quality and artistic merit – from Paul Iribe's lavish, coloured pochoir-printed designs for *Les Robes de Paul Poiret* (1908) to everyday newsprint – many fashion illustrations featured 'props' or scenic suggestions that reinforced

the fashion aesthetic or alluded to the occasions and contexts within which the clothes might be worn. Lucile's fashion album was, in contrast, garment-specific: it had to convey cut, detailing, novelty and originality, and the prospective client's eye could not be distracted. This strategy could be likened to the ploy Lucile adopted within her fashion houses, which were uniformly decorated pale grey, with her staff clothed also in pale grey, in order to foreground her fashion designs. Whilst discreetly painted jewellery signifies occasion and status, pictorial narrative is rare: when it does appear it is subtle, such as the hand that clasps a letter in the illustration on page 44. Otherwise, a mood or situation is evoked textually by Lucile's imaginative choice of dress names.

The fashion artist drew a silhouette of the figure prior to 'dressing' it. This period predates the vogue for elongated fashion bodies: the figures depicted in Lucile's album correspond to the height of the natural body, which is the combined length of six or seven heads. The bodies are positioned to show the clothing designs to best advantage. Many are half or slightly turned to display a side and front view of an ensemble. One arm is bent to permit observation of the construction of the dress and sleeve, as well as the position of the minimized, corseted waist. What is perhaps unusual about Lucile's album is the meticulous and detailed rendition of the faces and, most notably, the piercing eyes which frequently gaze directly at the viewer. It was customary for the fashion face to be rendered simply, with eyes cast away, in order to foreground the clothes. This 'defiance' is perfectly in keeping with Lucile's choice of risqué garment names and designs that were simultaneously seductive and empowering.

A fashion artist needed a technical understanding of how clothes were cut and constructed, the qualities of different fabrics and how garments interfaced with the feminine body. Their job involved translating a three-dimensional garment, mounted on a dress stand, into two dimensions, whilst striking a careful balance between detail and simplification, literal truth and suggestion. Presenting the qualities of the staggering array of fashionable fabrics and trimmings in paint and ink also demanded sensitivity and skill. In a contemporary magazine article fashion artist S.E. Bell advised readers interested in entering this profession that silk and silk satin were best shown by a 'slick and sharp' treatment of lights, darks and half-tones, whilst lace should be depicted by highlighting and slightly exaggerating the pattern. For three-dimensional fabric flowers, which Lucile adored and used profusely, the writer advised, 'When they are massed, the general light and shade should be blocked in; then a few flowers picked out and carefully worked up.'[2] Comparative analysis with the surviving dress reveals that this is precisely what the fashion artist did when she painted the rosebuds on 'Carresaute' (see page 89 and page 181).

Once completed, Lucile's fashion album formed a valued business document. Copying was rife within the industry and, on occasion, Lucile herself was not immune to its temptations. In turn, her album would have provided a wealth of references for a less talented dressmaker to exploit. Stuck to the front cover of the album is a printed label which reads 'From LUCILE Ltd. Autumn 1905. 23, Hanover Square London W.' – such multi-purpose labels indicated ownership, a 'security tag' when the valuable album was sent out to a trustworthy (it was hoped), highly valued existing, or potential, client.

Usual practice for a fashion house involved sending designs on single sheets to clients. It was exciting to discover in the Lucile Archive, donated to the V&A in the 1960s, single plates of designs identical to those in the 1905 album, acquired in 1986. These reveal that the fashion artist was required to paint multiples of some designs, probably those predicted to be most popular. On the reverse of these is a warning of a penalty fee of 7s.6d. incurred for non-return, which confirms that they were sent to press and clients.

Upon receiving the bound volume – in Lucile's salon or in private – the potential client first glimpsed its cover. As Lucile was so concerned with the overall look of the dressed feminine body, it is perhaps surprising that she did not decorate the cover of the 1905 album to render it distinctly 'Lucile' – to set a mood prior to it being opened. The client's response to the album – how they would 'read' it – was obviously key to a potential sale; here a further parallel with the photograph album is useful. Edwards observed that photograph albums are acknowledged to have a narrative that is unique to the individual reader, and the same could be said for Lucile's album, both in its material form and as a facsimile presented here. Each viewer determines their own 'track', '…those pages lingered over, those skipped over, investing the object with narrative …interwoven with private fantasy…'[3] Absence – or immateriality – can also fire the imagination: one page in Lucile's album is blank apart from the provocative, hand-inked, title 'Passionate Thought'…

The items that form the Lucile Archive at the V&A were valued and safeguarded from the outset. Even though Lucile's houses were geographically dispersed and her role within the business tumultuous

Detail from *From Lucile Ltd. Autumn 1905*. Arms were depicted bent to maximize the reader's view of the cut and fabrication of the garment offered for sale.

ABOVE AND RIGHT Two ink line drawings of a Lucile ensemble reveal how different fashion artists responded to the same ensemble, 1912–13.

towards the end, during the course of her career she amassed and preserved a significant quantity of design-related documents. Disinterested in company administration, it was her creative accomplishments that she prized and preserved.

At some point, possibly when Lucile moved into a nursing home or shortly after she died, the Archive passed into the care of her family. In her private life and professional existence, Lucile had sometimes disregarded social convention, to the chagrin of some of her relatives. Considering these records were accorded almost no cultural, historical or financial value during the 1930s, it is perhaps remarkable that her family kept them. In fact, Lucile's descendants carefully housed the legacy of her working life for over three decades. At the very point at which their value was about to shift into the realm of serious, desirable, fashion history, her grandson, the late Earl of Halsbury, FRS, generously donated them to the V&A. In contrast to the Archive, the 1904 and 1905 fashion albums had somehow entered the public domain and could have suffered a terrible fate.

During the 1950s and 1960s, Lucile's fashion albums would have attracted scant attention, their importance recognized only amidst a coterie of dress historians, specialist collectors and curators. By the 1970s, when the importance of fashion and its representation was becoming increasingly widely recognized (culturally and to a degree financially), the albums might have been broken up (as so many were) and sold profitably as individual plates. Most fortunately, the survival of the albums in an intact state was ensured by Doris Langley Moore, OBE, FRSL (1902–1989). In addition to being a leading Byron scholar, Mrs Langley Moore was a pioneer collector of historical fashion and its representation. In 1963 the Museum of Costume in Bath was founded to house her extensive collection. Mrs Langley Moore was especially interested in fashion imagery as a source of dress-historical evidence: her book *Fashion through Fashion Plates* (1971) instantly became a standard reference for dress historians. We do not know where or when she acquired the Lucile albums but we do know they formed part of her personal reference library. Much of her contextual fashion material was housed in the Fashion Study Centre which she established: an innovative archive located near to the Museum to provide contextual material for researchers.

Shortly before her death, this significant library was divided up and offered for sale at Christie's, South Kensington: it was believed to be the first sale of a library devoted to the study of fashion.[4] The auction comprised 237 lots, which included groups of plates and fashion publications dating from the 1770s to 1980. Whilst most items for sale were printed works, the Lucile albums were unique and were listed separately in the catalogue. Item 171 was described thus: 'Lucile, original designs in watercolour with samples of the materials and trimmings in which they were carried out for *Lucile Ltd, 23 Hanover Square, London W.,* 48 designs for Autumn 1904, 69 designs for Autumn 1905, 2 vols., American cloth, 1904 and 1905. (est £2–4,000)'. Curators working in the Textiles Collection at the V&A ('Dress' was not yet part of the title) instantly recognized their value as historical objects of major significance for multiple discourses and disciplines, including dress history, and as an extraordinary, inspirational, visual reference for many, including fashion and theatre designers.

By 1986 surviving Edwardian fashionable dress was fragile, rare and had risen in commercial value. Lucile's role within fashion and broader

The Lucile Archive contains a number of partially completed designs. This pencil drawing from 1904 outlines a fashionable silhouette prior to the dressing of the body.

Lucile

Photograph (rear view) of a model wearing the ensemble 'Ishkoodah' and a print of an ink line drawing depicting the front view of the same suit, which is similarly accessorized.

By *c.*1912 Lucile had commissioned a Parisian photographic studio to print multiples of hand-drawn designs. Each print was embossed to give it an aura of exclusivity and deter fashion piracy.

This near-complete, annotated fashion drawing, also from 1904, depicts the feminine body clothed, but requires more detail. The artist has worked on one sleeve, which in its layered detail is unequivocally hallmarked Lucile. The same pose appears regularly in Lucile's Autumn 1905 album.

A touch of violet-coloured watercolour has been daubed upon a pencil drawing of a shepherdess-style ensemble of 1904.

cultural history was an acknowledged fact and her luxurious clothes were represented in major international dress collections. Surviving garments enhance our knowledge of the designs, palette and materials she favoured and indicate a client's preferences – clothes they selected, ordered and were subsequently made to fit their unique shape perfectly. A few gowns possessed exceptional 'biographies', such as the Lucile clothes worn by famous modern dancer and beauty Irene Castle (now at the Costume Institute) or by private client Heather Firbank (at the V&A *see page 212*). They have layers of meaning – who wore them, where and when. It was recognized that the albums offered new insights into Lucile's design and working practice. The albums also suggested other possibilities within the context of museum collections and archives. In the V&A, they could, for example, be compared with *Barbara Johnson's Album of Fashion and Fabrics*, a personal fashion album, compiled almost 160 years previously by young, fashion-aware Barbara Johnson. For her compendium, made between 1746 and 1823, she painstakingly assembled printed fashion plates and fabric swatches, accompanied by hand-written notes on her various fashion purchases and the reasons for her choices.[5]

With the support and genuine enthusiasm of Sir Roy Strong, former Museum Director, the two Lucile albums were 'won' by the V&A and their future secured. Once the albums entered the Museum context their financial value seemed immaterial: they became unique (invaluable) objects of fashion history, possessing new attributes that were first and foremost interpretative and inspirational.

The entry of fashionable clothes by Lucile (and by other designers) into museum collections is often serendipitous. With only limited purchase funds available for modern fashionable dress, the majority of public collections are donations-led. However, funds are made available in exceptional circumstances, such as the purchasing of these albums and the dress 'Carresaute' in 2007. This comprehensive seasonal collection of Lucile's designs is extraordinary – the albums give a detailed picture of the range of garments, fabrics and colours deemed sartorially correct for a wealthy, fashionable woman to wear during the inclement weather of Autumn 1905. When it was acquired the 1905 album was especially fragile and was prioritized for conservation, and is thus now the stronger of the two. As the production of this publication involved handling and photography, it was selected to form the focus of the book rather than the 1904 album.

The album comprises 69 ensembles: four are illustrated with different bodices or shown with and without a jacket. For day wear, there are tailored walking costumes and visiting ensembles, mostly made in woollen cloth; afternoon gowns, in glistening silk velvet and rustling silk taffeta; and one motoring coat made in protective wool. There are designs for 25 evening dresses and four ball or opera gowns composed of confections of luxurious, filmy and pliant dressmaking fabrics. The remaining designs depict two opera coats and one peignoir, the latter being the only intimate garment. Whereas today an outfit might require just two or three fabrics and a very limited number of trimmings, this album reveals that it was not uncommon for Lucile to use nine or ten textiles – sometimes more – together with a plethora of trimmings. The Autumn 1905 album also makes explicit Lucile's enduring preference for fabrics dyed blue, purple, pink and green, together with their numerous tonal variants.

This loose-sheet watercolour design, from the Archive, depicts the first ensemble in Lucile's Autumn 1905 album.

Throughout her career Lucile's designs were drawn and painted, with fabric swatches attached. This *garçonne* design dates from the late 1920s, when she worked as 'Lucy Duff Gordon Ltd' from premises in New Bond Street, London.

With reference to her early years as a dressmaker, Lucile wrote: 'My first clients chose their dresses from sketches which I drew for them, and these were never copied for any other woman.'[6] The Archive provides evidence of her own fashion designs and reveals that, when business was brisk, she engaged fashion artists to assist her. An assessment of the range of work housed in the Archive reveals that Lucile championed new technological developments to document, publicize and disseminate her designs. She exploited the realism and opportunity for multiple images that photography could provide, installed her own photo studios and used her salons and gardens as elegant locations.

The Archive contains numerous examples of loose sheets of ink and shaded pencil drawings of Lucile's designs that were sent out to clients and press, including multiple drawings of the same garment. Later, Lucile had her designs replicated in multiple copies, a cost-effective solution requiring just one original artwork. A group of 23 ink drawings on card, *c.*1910–11, have tiny handwritten pencil annotations with print specifications, such as '16 copies. 6½". 2 on painting paper. 4 on card'.

In 1905 Lucile's album was a unique working document that contained evidence of a season's creativity and was a prized business asset. Today, it is cherished and safeguarded as an historical rarity. This facsimile now makes it widely accessible for interpretation and inspiration. Would Lucile have approved? Almost certainly!

The dimensions of the original album are 305mm height by 245mm width. Within the album there are two sets of erratic pagination, one written in 1905 and the pencil notes most likely added by the auction house at the point of sale. Some blank double page spreads have been deleted for the purpose of this reproduction.

The Facsimile

From LUCILE Ltd.

Autumn. 1905.

23, Hanover Square, London, W.

N.º 50

FROM
JOHN STAIT,
323, OXFORD STREET,
Account Book Manufacturer,
PRINTER &c.

LEDGERS, DAY BOOKS, CASH & BILL BOOKS.
A LARGE ASSORTMENT IN STOCK.

Every Description of Account Books made on the Premises
at the Shortest Notice.

1a

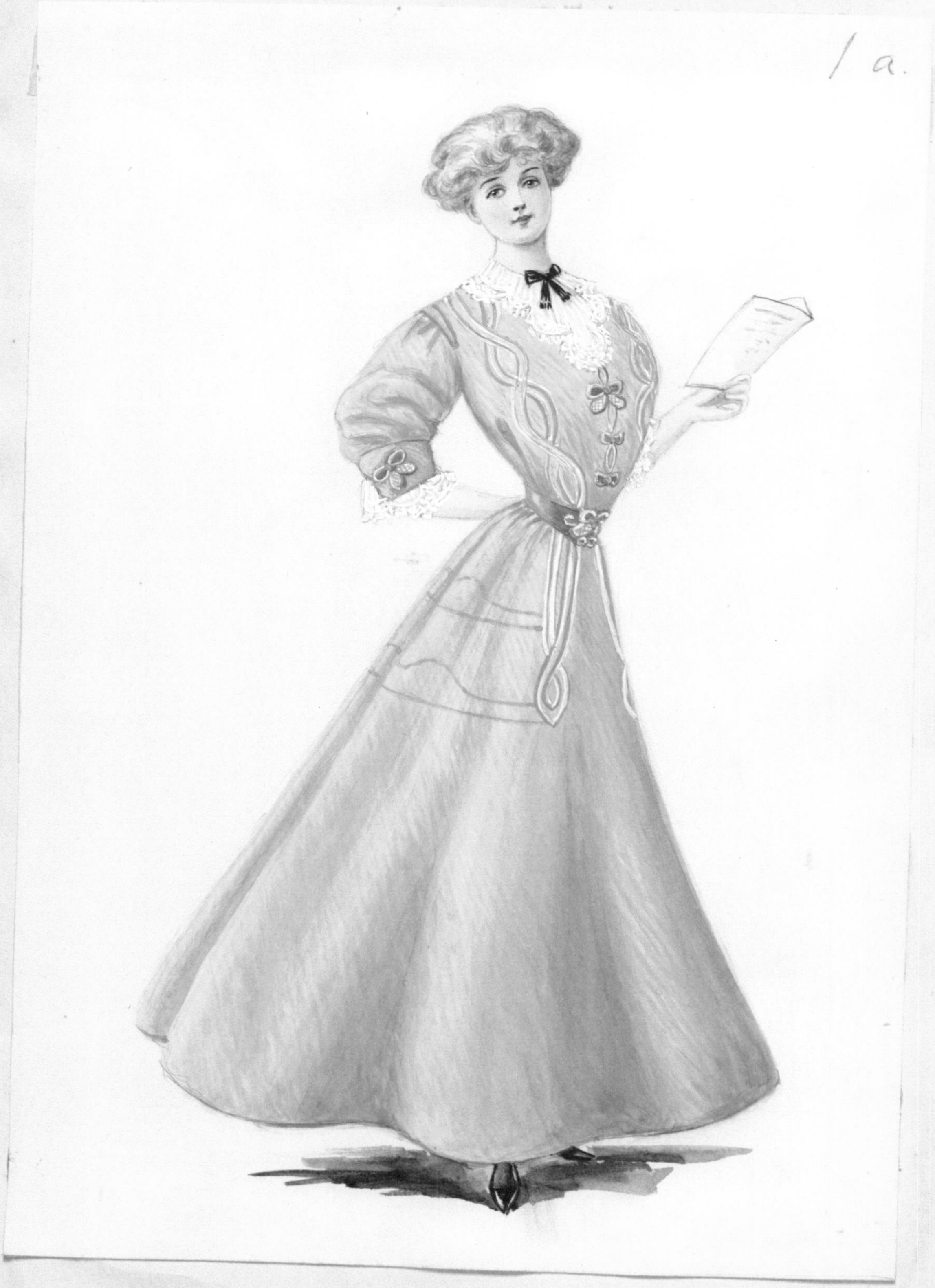

2

2 2.

2a

2

3.

4

5.

50.

10

11

42 11

12.

"The tender grace of a day that is dead."

13

16

16

17

17

18.

18.

18.W

"Cynthia"

21

"*Melisande.*"

22

23

24.

"Carresaute".

27 a.

"Faule des Roses"

27

27

"A Protest."

28

"Eldorado."

"Illusion."

30.

"Illusion."

"A transient beauty."

" Love while you may."

32

33

"When life's young pleasure's woo."

"Intention"

35

"The shortness of time."

36

"Madame Elizabeth."

37.

"The Sweetness of Love."

38.

"Daphne."

39.

"Revelry"

"Climax"

41

"An episode"

43.

45

45

"Passionate Thought"

"Passionate Thought"

47

"Farewell Summer."

53

53

54

54

5-5

5-6

59

59

"Because."

62.

"Enrapture"

63.

"Oblivion."

65

"Unforgotten"

67

68.

68

"L'Allegro."

45.

70

73.

"The Moment"

From Lucile Ltd. Autumn 1905. Notes on the Album

PP.43 & 44 WALKING COSTUME, AND AFTERNOON ENSEMBLE, JACKET, BODICE, SKIRT, HAT AND MUFF

A fitted jacket in pale turquoise soft woollen twill fastens with a passementerie motif. The front panels have intertwined lines of soutache and a triangular cut-away revealing a lace blouse. Wide, bracelet-length sleeves are gathered below narrow epaulettes and into cuffs trimmed with lines of soutache and edged in satin and ermine. A short ermine tie emerges from a stand-up collar circled by a wide blue ribbon and bow. The matching flared skirt has lines of soutache and clears the ground, revealing pointed black glacé kid shoes. A soft, low toque of turquoise wool bordered in ermine is trimmed with a black bow and pink silk flowers. A matching muff has ruched trimming and bands of ermine.

For indoor wear with the same skirt, a fitted bodice has a high, round neck and a lace-edged pleated tulle jabot with black silk bow. It centre-front fastens beneath applied bows flanked by intertwined lines of soutache. Wide elbow-length sleeves are gathered under small epaulettes and into cuffs trimmed with bows. Lace frills protrude beyond the cuffs. The hatless mannequin holds a folded letter. These 'short' skirts (just clearing the ground) were described in French as *trotteuse*, or *trottoir*. In 1903 *The Queen* described the style as 'the trotting skirt meant for morning shopping, walking and country pursuits'. They were lighter and easier to wear than skirts with hampering trains.

PP.45 & 46 WALKING COSTUME AND AFTERNOON ENSEMBLE, JACKET, BODICE, SKIRT AND HAT

Over a lace blouse with stock collar, a short, boxy, double-breasted jacket in beige soft woollen twill has revers faced with blue silk velvet and edged with brown fur. It has a deep yoke and scalloped-edged lower panels, and fastens with four buttons. Wide, bracelet-length sleeves are eased into the shoulders and pleated into cuffs trimmed with velvet and fur. Decorative touches include lined, slashed darts at the inner arms and bold top-stitching. The matching flared skirt has top-stitched pleats and a crenellated line of soutache above the hem. To aid mobility, it is several inches above the ground, revealing black glacé kid shoes. A low toque in blue velvet edged with fur and trimmed with pink roses has a thrown-back, brown lace veil.

For afternoon wear, the same skirt is teamed with a pleated, fitted, single-breasted bodice with silver-rimmed buttons and gigot sleeves. Beneath is a lace blouse with stand-up collar and lace jabot tied with a black ribbon bow with fancy pendants. A shaped belt (edged in blue) fastens with a large oval silver buckle.

'No Frenchwoman will commit the folly of trailing around the muddy street in a long garment.' *The Lady's Realm*, November 1903

P.47 ENSEMBLE FOR COUNTRY WEAR, BODICE, SKIRT AND HAT

A fitted Norfolk-style bodice in red-brown soft woollen twill has a high round neck with a small pointed collar over a blouse with a high, turn-over, lace-edged collar. The single-breasted garment is fastened with a row of gilt buttons flanked by pleats and applied bands with small patch pockets. Gigot sleeves have forearms trimmed with buttons. The bodice fits below a belt fastened with straps and gilt buckles. The matching skirt has a pair of applied bands with buttoned-down points. The skirt is a few inches above the ground, revealing pointed black glacé kid shoes. A mannish brown felt hat with a flat crown is trimmed with long pheasant quills.

'But surely it is in the worst possible taste to wear pitiable bits and pieces of the very birds about to be slaughtered? One girl sports an entire pheasant trail in her hat: another a head, all complete with beak and glass eyes.' Lady Cynthia Asquith, *Remember and be Glad*, 1952 (p.130)

P.49 WALKING OR VISITING ENSEMBLE, JACKET, SKIRT AND HAT

Over a white blouse trimmed with a black bow, the short, single-breasted jacket in pewter-grey wool has pointed fronts edged in white decorated with lines of soutache. It fastens with a bow of black military braid. Wide, bracelet-length sleeves are eased into the shoulders and gathered into deep cuffs. Revers, hem and cuffs are trimmed with gold braid and ovals of bright orange satin. The flared skirt grazes the ground and pleats at the waist are emphasized by soutache. A peach-orange 'bowler' hat has an upturned brim and crown with a black ribbon band passing through a gilt buckle. A black veil is worn over the face.

'The best veils are of fine mesh with chenille spots of various sizes thereon. The disfiguring spots of abnormal size have, thank goodness, become démodé'. *The Lady's Realm*, December 1901

P.51 COSTUME, JACKET, SKIRT AND HAT

In dark-green velvet, the short, fitted, single-breasted bodice has layered collars in black and green and turned-back front edges trimmed with black braid and yellow mimosa sprigs. Wide, bracelet-length sleeves are gathered into cuffs banded in green and black enlivened with mimosa sprigs. The matching skirt with narrow *tablier* front is secured by a belt with yellow trimming and falls to a short train. Both garments have a diamond trellis of applied military braid in different widths broken by bands of horizontally applied braid. In the *New York American Examiner* (1910) Lucile described a garment as 'braided to death'. A small black hat trimmed with black *coq* wings has a crown covered with a veil of bright-green tulle (edged with black lace).

'Hideous green gauze veils... no woman in her right mind will countenance such an absurdity.' *The Woman at Home*, April– November 1901 (p.456)

P.53 WALKING COSTUME, JACKET, SKIRT AND HAT

In muted grey-brown soft woollen twill, the fitted, single-breasted jacket (worn over a blouse with an upright collar trimmed with a mauve bow) has a high round neck and a centre-front of white wool with crenellated lines of gold soutache. Bodice fronts are ornamented with crenellated lines of dark soutache. Long, gigot sleeves have cuffs of white wool elaborated with soutache and braid. The matching skirt is held in place by a belt with gilt buckle and has a centre front inverted pleat. It flares to touch the ground and has lines of soutache echoing the bodice decoration. One dainty, pointed black glacé kid shoe peeps out under the skirt. A brown, low-crowned hat with a pink ribbon band threaded through a diamanté buckle has a thrown-back brown veil secured at the back in wide cartridge pleats.

Wired velvet bandeaux could be sewn into rims to raise hats high above the head, then dangerously long hat pins (with safety guards) were stuck through hats and hair to secure the towering edifices at a fashionable forward tilt.

P.55 VISITING COSTUME, BODICE, SKIRT AND HAT

In black velvet and taffeta, the fitted bodice has a stomacher enclosed by ornate black military braid. Bracelet-length sleeves have braid appliqué and cuffs of silver braid adorned with gold gimp. A short ermine tie hangs about the neck over a blouse with an upright collar and bow trim around its top edge. A belt of silver braid is embellished with gold gimp. With a long train, the matching skirt has elaborate black braid trimming. A pink hat covered with clustered pink flowers and cartridge-pleated ribbons has a thrown-back black spotted tulle veil over a pink silk cascade. Decorative braids and ruched bands had to be applied meticulously (to achieve symmetry) and with restraint, as they could make an ensemble exceedingly heavy. Mrs Evan Nepean condemned weight in dress 'as one of the seventy-seven deadly sartorial sins' (*The Queen*, October 1904).

P.57 WALKING ENSEMBLE, JACKET, SKIRT AND HAT

In dark olive-green woollen cloth the short, fitted Zouave jacket (trimmed with rows of tiny enamel buttons and edged with spangled white twill) is open over a lace blouse with a purple velvet bow and pendants with gilt tags. Long gigot sleeves have cuffs banded with white wool, purple velvet and gold braid. Fronts and sleeves have a linear design (inspired by Hungarian embroidery) applied in black soutache. The matching skirt is gathered beneath a shaped belt and is trimmed with soutache and braid in a design echoing the bodice. An awkwardly drawn, trained lower skirt (in identical wool) appears to be a later addition to lengthen the ensemble. A purple hat with side-swept brim is trimmed with long black quills and has a black, fancy-edged, spotted tulle veil lowered over the face. A slender umbrella completes the ensemble.

'In addition to her effort to resuscitate coloured veils *La mode* did a very cruel thing when she decreed patterned lace veils de rigueur. These were worn by all sorts and conditions of women, and, with a few exceptions, had the very worst effect, for they made the wearer look as if she were disfigured by unsightly burns or the tattoo markings of an Indian chieftain.' Mrs Eric Pritchard, *The Cult of Chiffon*, 1902 (p.180)

P.58 WALKING ENSEMBLE, REDINGOTE (COAT), SKIRT AND HAT

Over a white blouse with jabot and blue bow, the long, fitted coat in sludge-green woollen cloth has notched revers and is closed with three graduated buttoned down tabs. Bracelet-length sleeves swell over the elbows then are gathered into cuffs fastened with silver buttons. Top-stitched tucks along the inner arm shape the sleeves. Lower coat panels are moulded tightly over the hips and flare in smooth lines to below the knees. The matching, trained skirt is edged with brown fur. A brown 'bowler' hat with a white band and gilt buckle is trimmed with white flowers while a fancy-edged, spotted tulle veil shields the face.

'I would here impress upon my readers the mistake that is made by short women wearing a three quarter length coat with a short skirt. Even a tall woman can hardly afford to cut her figure in this wise.' *The Lady's Realm*, November 1904

P.59 VISITING GOWN, JACKET, SKIRT AND HAT

In dark-purple woollen cloth, the short bolero has narrow front panels edged with scalloped black silk machine lace. It opens over a white, bow-trimmed blouse (with lace cascade) and corselette banded in three shades of purple. Revers of bright magenta velvet have gold gilt motifs laced through with pendants of black braid embellished with tiny gold gilt pom-poms. Wide, elbow-length sleeves are gathered into magenta velvet cuffs (with perky bows) edged with black lace. The purple cloth skirt is moulded over the hips and falls to a short train. It has an applied self band that curves above the hem, divides and snakes up the centre front (*see page 184*). The black hat has a low, fur-trimmed crown and slightly curved brim adorned with black lace frills (ending in streamers) and purple silk flowers.

A lady's maid had the tiresome job of keeping clothes clean. Mud on the skirt could be brushed off when dry, little localized stains could be dabbed away carefully with cleaning agents or treated with applications of dry bran or breadcrumbs; if all else failed, expensive professional dry cleaners existed. Warnings were sounded about the dangers of dry-cleaning at home – highly volatile liquids had to be used outdoors to avoid the risk of fire or explosion.

P.61 AFTERNOON ENSEMBLE, JACKET AND SKIRT

In pale blue woollen cloth, the short, fitted jacket has an asymmetrical front fastened with two outsize buttons. Its decorative top is formed of alternating bands of lace, metallic fabric and embroidered taffeta with cloth revers. Short sleeves are gathered at the shoulders and have U-shaped cut-outs through which sleeves of tightly packed chiffon frills protrude. A plain matching skirt is gathered beneath a shaped belt and drapes to a short train. Blonde hair is arranged in a popular winged style over an array of false pieces, transformations and mesh supports.

'Celebrated wood-engraver Gwen Raverat lamented that, in her childhood, hair 'had to be puffed out in hideous lumps and bumps over cushions or frames'. *Period Piece*, 1952 (p.261)

P.63 VISITING ENSEMBLE, JACKET, SKIRT AND HAT

In royal purple woollen cloth, the fitted jacket is slit open to the waist over a white blouse with an upright collar. A spatula-shaped lace rabat is trimmed with a black bow and laces embellished with gold-gilt tags. Edged with mid-purple velvet, the front panels have borders of velvet and decorative applied braid. Wide, three-quarter sleeves are full over the elbows and have purple velvet cuffs. Lace blouse sleeves reach beyond the wrists. A matching skirt is eased into the waist beneath an ornate, shaped belt of gilt leaves. The centre-front skirt is decorated to thigh-level with lines of soutache and tabs (echoed at sleeve heads, cuffs and bodice fronts). A hat with a purple brim and a ruffled black satin crown is trimmed with raven quills secured by a gilt Art Nouveau buckle. A black-spotted tulle veil is worn over the face. This minuscule figure has a defiant stance, emphasized by her hat's upright quills. In her autobiography, Lucile recollected that she was one of the first to oppose the wanton and cruel use of plumage in millinery, and by promoting ribbon-trimmed hats she helped the bird preservation movement.

P.65 'THE TENDER GRACE OF A DAY THAT IS DEAD' ENSEMBLE, BODICE, SKIRT AND HAT

Over a lace blouse with an upright collar and cascade, the high-waisted bodice has pendant-flared edges of dark green velvet. Side panels of semi-transparent green silk chiffon over the blouse (scattered with pink silk rosebuds) have matching short sleeves gathered into velvet cuffs bordered with brown fur. Lace puffs and frills emerge below the cuffs. Chiffon panels have deep borders of gold gilt braid threaded with pale blue, white and mauve rouleaux, which emerge as a looped rosette over a central fancy gilt bow fastening. In dark green woollen cloth, the lower bodice (with cut-away front) is moulded tightly over the figure to hip level. The long, matching wool skirt with train has top-stitched pleats and is edged with brown fur. A low-crowned dark green felt hat (worn perched over the brow) has a pale green silk chiffon band (ending in streamers) and a circle of mauve, purple, white and green flowers. A gold lorgnette is held in the right hand. Twenty fabric samples and trimmings enclose the design. Lucile wrote: 'I pick and choose from many fabrics and laces and trimmings and I build up a beautiful toilette that is truly artistic… .' (*New York American Examiner*, 1910)

P.69 VISITING ENSEMBLE, BODICE, SKIRT AND HAT

In dark brown wool *barège*, the short, draped bodice with cut-away front is worn over a white and pink lace blouse with an upright collar and narrow cascade. Just below the neck, dark brown velvet strapping fastens across the bodice from shoulder to shoulder. Elbow-length sleeves have double puffs and lace-edged cuffs that open over long, elaborate blouse sleeves. The matching *barège* skirt is gathered beneath a shaped belt in two shades of pink taffeta and silver tissue. Trimmed with horizontal dark brown strapping, the skirt has a short train. A dusky pink hat has a low crown circled by a cartridge-pleated frill and pale pink rosebuds. A black bow secures the black, spotted tulle veil, which cascades at the back.

'Brown, again, may be expressed in many materials, though I do not like it in alpaca, éolienne and face cloth; yet I love brown silk or satin especially in the dead leaf tones…' Mrs Evan Nepean, 'The Placing of Colours', *The Queen*, August 1904

P.71 AFTERNOON COSTUME, BODICE, SKIRT AND HAT

Over a button-trimmed lace blouse with stand-up collar, the fitted bodice (in bright blue silk velvet) has a narrow, U-shaped neckline gathered round the neck by crossed laces with dangling gilt tassels. Short puffed velvet sleeves are set in under epaulettes and lace gigot sleeves extend to the wrists. The matching velvet skirt is secured by a black belt with gold gilt buckle. It is gathered at centre-front, and back panels are lapped over each side in curved, piped seams. A pale blue hat has an upturned brim trimmed with matching ostrich feathers. A black lace veil swathes around the crown and drapes at the back.

'Little gold tags and tassels and silken pendants of all descriptions appear on dresses of voile and alpaca…' 'A Vista of Fashion', Mrs Aria, *The Queen*, March 1902

P.73 AFTERNOON RECEPTION GOWN, BODICE AND SKIRT

In mid-brown velvet, the bodice is open-fronted and cross-laced in wide, pale blue-grey ribbon (trimmed with twisted lines of silver gilt) over a lace blouse with a funnel collar that falls over the shoulders. Gathered velvet sleeves flare widely to the elbows and deep lace cuffs are tied with blue-grey ribbon and edged with fur. In matching velvet the skirt is gathered beneath a silver belt with gold braid trim. It has a train and is decorated with triple horizontal lines at hip-level. Velvet was popular for the Autumn/Winter season 1905, as designers appreciated its becoming sheen, sensual texture and graceful, draping qualities. Quoting from historical dress, using cross-lacing, voluminous sleeves, deep lace collar and cuffs, Lucile created a 'picturesque' gown – a speciality of the firm.

PP.74 & 75 VISITING ENSEMBLE, BODICE, SKIRT, PÉLERINE, MUFF AND HAT

The pale turquoise-green gown is shown here with accessories for outdoor wear. A ruched black silk velvet pélerine has a V neckline reaching to the waist over an infill with an upright collar and rows of ruffled lace – it ties with pastel-coloured chiné ribbon bows. A large matching velvet muff has ruffled ends bordered with ermine. The black picture hat has a wide brim trimmed with a cartridge-pleated ruffle and fly-away tailored bow.

In fine, pale turquoise-green wool, the bodice has a high neckline with a V-neck, flat, lace collar, threaded through with pale blue ribbon and trimmed with ribbon flowers. An embroidered plastron is edged with frilled turquoise lace. Over long lace sleeves, gathered bracelet-length sleeves have double puffs. The matching skirt (softly pleated beneath an ornate green and gold belt) has a spangled *tablier* front and drapes to a short train. Max Rivière (writing in *Femina*, in January 1905, with tongue in cheek) described muffs as portable cupboards for a multitude of objects from handkerchiefs to newspapers, claiming that in 12 years they had lengthened from a diminutive 10cm to a capacious 60cm.

P.77 'CYNTHIA' VISITING ENSEMBLE, BODICE, SKIRT AND HAT

In mauve wool, velvet and taffeta embellished with covered domed buttons, the short bodice is worn over a lace blouse with an upright collar trimmed with a pale blue silk bow with streamers. Crossed bands create a wide, low, V neckline (lace-edged) and cut-away front. Diamond panels are gathered over the bust. Three-quarter sleeves have fullness over the elbows and button-trimmed, lace-edged cuffs open over tight, wrist-length blouse sleeves. A matching mauve skirt is gathered below a shaped self belt and drapes gracefully to a short train. A low-crowned boater in diaphanous black has ruched black ribbon around the brim and crown, and a tailored bow with a streamer trims the back.

Queen Alexandra was particularly fond of mauve and many followed her lead. In her autobiography, Lucile remembered '…women who made an art of beautiful dressing. The late Countess of Dudley was one of them. I can see her now, walking slowly and with that very graceful gait of hers into my showroom, her dress of mauve chiffon falling in a cloud of draperies to her little feet… .'

P.79 VISITING ENSEMBLE, JACKET, SKIRT AND HAT

In russet taffeta and velvet, the single-breasted, short jacket has a low V neckline (with revers) fastened with a single bow. It has a deep border of frilled lace and blue ribbon dotted with yellow rosebuds. The front panels have a dark pink lace overlay. Bouffant, elbow-length sleeves are gathered into spool-shaped cuffs with silver and gold metal lace trim. A white lace blouse has a stand-up collar with a white bow and bracelet-length sleeves threaded with pale blue ribbon. The matching taffeta skirt (with long train) is gathered beneath a silver belt with a diamond-shaped buckle. It has a row of bows down the centre front, applied diagonal bands of dark pink lace and a velvet border. The black hat, with a silver and gold band, has a frilled lace brim, a black bow with streamers and a cluster of blue flowers.

'Entire toilettes of brown are very effective if the different shades are well blended.' *The Lady*, January 1905

P.81 'MELISANDE' EVENING GOWN, BODICE AND SKIRT

In purple-blue silk brocaded with a floral trefoil design in yellow, green and pink, the bodice, with short puff sleeves, has an off-the-shoulder, plunging, low décolletage edged with blue velvet. It is worn over a lace chemisette with frilled sleeves. The elongated bodice front is decorated with an *échelle* of blue velvet ribbon bows. A matching brocade skirt (with short train) falls in soft pleats and the centre-front *échelle* of ribbon bows is continued to the hem (bordered with blue velvet). Tasselled ends of a long (unfastened) rope of pearls are held by delicately painted hands. White chemisettes with tiny frills of washable lace or muslin provided flattering frames for the head and shoulders and prevented perspiration, body oils and make-up soiling non-washable bodices.

P.83 ENSEMBLE, BODICE, SKIRT AND HAT

In purple-blue brocade, the bodice, worn over a lace blouse with V neckline, has a centre-front *échelle* of ribbon bows and three-quarter blue velvet sleeves with lace cuffs. The skirt is the same as shown on page 81. A draped blue chiffon open-fronted robe is worn over the ensemble. It has a steep V neckline, elbow-length sleeves and long handkerchief points, and is edged throughout in brown fur. A gold metallic fabric belt with oval buckle circles the waist. A pale blue hat has an upturned brim trimmed with matching ostrich feathers. A black lace veil swathes around the crown and drapes at the back.

P.85 OPERA OR THEATRE COAT
In bright turquoise woollen plush, the capacious *saque* garment has a high, round neck with black 'Peter Pan' collar and a narrow, U-shaped plastron trimmed with loops and buttons. The smock-like front has an ornate linear pattern in gold soutache. Wide, long sleeves are eased into dropped shoulders and have deep cuffs, edged with black fur and trimmed with gold soutache. Over a trained black skirt, the calf-length garment flares to a wide hem with short vertical slits embellished with gold soutache to match bodice and cuffs. Front edges are trimmed with lines of gold soutache. One well-dressed socialite was known to confine her evening gowns to black and white, and 'let herself go' in audacious and expensive 'cloaks'. This deep piled wool kept a winter opera-goer warm, whereas in summer an opera coat became 'a costly trifle of flounced chiffon, lace, jewelled trimming and endless garlands of artificial flowers – a thing of beauty and of price.' (*The Woman at Home*, April-September 1901, p.553)

P.87 MOTORING COAT
In bright tomato-red and white wool faced cloth, the single-breasted voluminous *saque* coat (resembling a Carrick, or 'triple decker') has wide sleeves set in below a triple-tiered cape. The collar, white wool revers and sleeve insets are decorated with applied diamond motifs in ecru taffeta, gold and black soutache and black military braid. The coat fastens with diamond-shaped frogging and tasselled ties. Ostentatious motoring coats such as this were worn on special occasions, but for everyday 'automobiling' it was usual to cover up with a beige silk tussore or holland dust coat, or waterproof overcoat.

P.89 'CARRESAUTE' EVENING GOWN, BODICE AND SKIRT
In pale turquoise blue chiffon over an ecru satin foundation, the bodice has a low, wide décolletage with slightly pouched front and short frilled sleeves. The neckline is edged with lace and chiffon frills over a row of tiny pink silk gauze roses; three larger pink roses mark the cleavage. Metal strip embroidery glistens through the chiffon over the bust (outlined by curving bands of finely ruched chiffon). A silver and white belt has two long

tasselled streamers. The matching trained skirt has horizontal flounces of chiffon, overlaid bands of lace and a broad band of shimmering metal embroidery. Frail concoctions such as this often 'suffered catastrophic damage at dances. I would recognize some wisp of material swathed around a pair of feet at the other side of the room as a fragment torn off my own frock.' (Lady Cynthia Asquith, *Remember and be Glad*, 1952, p.74)

P.90 VISITING OR AFTERNOON GOWN, BODICE, SKIRT AND HAT
A bodice of black silk with a multicoloured floral chiné pattern has an overlay of transparent purple silk. It has a steep V neckline (with Vandyked lace edging) that plunges to the waist over a white lace blouse with a demure round collar, low jabot and long sleeves with deep white lace cuffs. Narrow swathed sleeves are puffed at the elbows and edged with brown fur. The matching, slightly trained skirt (bordered with brown fur and purple velvet) is pleated beneath a shaped ornate gilt belt and has a filmy purple open-fronted over-skirt trimmed with ruching. A hat with side-swept brim and fur crown is ornamented with frilled black lace, purple and yellow silk flowers and lace streamers.
'Violet and pansy shades are also fashionable and the purple toque or hat trimmed with some shade of purple is met with everywhere' *The Lady*, January 1905

P.91 'FAUTE DES ROSES' DINNER OR EVENING GOWN, BODICE AND SKIRT
In the same fabrics as the design on page 90, the bodice has a deeply scooped neck (with pink borders and a purple bow) and short sleeves over a low, square-necked white chemisette with elbow-length sleeves trimmed with lace frills and gathered by green ribbon tied with bows.
It features the same ornate belt and skirt as above (without an overskirt).

P.93 'A PROTEST' EVENING GOWN, BODICE AND SKIRT
In striped taffeta (purple-blue, green and pink) with a chiné floral pattern, the fitted bodice has a low, off-the-shoulder neckline bordered with purple and green rouleaux within rows of lace and ruched bands of bright green silk. A scallop-edged lace chemisette is embroidered with silver bows and slotted with pale blue ribbon, and has puffed, elbow-length sleeves gathered by bright green ribbon tied in bows. Lines of rouleaux, a double row of domed buttons and a central ribbon rosette decorate the

lower bodice. The matching smooth-line, gored skirt has piped seams and a centre-front row of domed buttons. Seams are trimmed with rectangles of ruched and piped lines in bright green silk. Though she felt that the suffragette movement was 'a huge joke… a lot of nonsense and rather undignified', Lucile was not averse to exploiting its signature colours (purple, green and white) and naming this gown after suffrage demonstrations. She met and rather approved of Mrs Pankhurst, describing her in her autobiography as 'a dear little woman' (pp.99-100).

P.95 'ELDORADO' (ALSO CALLED 'MAKING A DEBUT') BALL OR OPERA GOWN, BODICE AND SKIRT
The bodice of bright pink challis over pink velvet has a plunging décolletage with a deep border of ruffled lace and gold-gilt braid extending down the centre front. The bodice is swathed into a twist (with tassels) over the cleavage and is clasped by a gilded, shaped belt with a large jewelled buckle. Below grey fur bands, wide sleeves of ruffled lace reach the elbows. The trained skirt is eased into the waist – the back panels are lapped over the sides in curved, top-stitched seams. Grey fur borders the skirt, but the fur sample pasted into the album has suffered over the years and is almost bald. 'Eldorado' is worn with a diamond and sapphire parure of tiara, necklace and drop earrings. 'These were the days of tiaras and stomachers. The blaze of jewels displayed at the opera was really amazing.' (George Cornwallis-West, *Edwardian Hey-Days*, 1930, p.129)

P.97 'ILLUSION' EVENING GOWN, BODICE AND SKIRT
The fitted bodice has a low, plunging neckline in pale turquoise blue tulle frosted with silver over a pale foundation. Insubstantial organza frills (caught by yellow silk roses) cover the shoulders. Over a camisole slotted with pale pink ribbon, the bodice side panels (edged with bold scrollwork in silver tissue) flank central scalloped cream and yellow embroidered panels. This decorative feature (trimmed with silk roses) is repeated down the front of the matching flounced overskirt. The waist is circled by two wide leaf-green ribbons. A trained foundation skirt has a silver scrollwork border.
'Smart frocks are showing a tremendous amount of flounces… It is in the graduation that the success or failure of a flounced skirt lies – an inch too short or too long in the front will ruin the whole effect.' *The Lady's Realm*, November 1903

P.99 'A TRANSIENT BEAUTY' EVENING GOWN, BODICE AND SKIRT
In spotted tulle over a pastel-green striped satin foundation, the lace-edged bodice has an off-the-shoulder neckline emphasized by lines of silver metallic braid that meander and intertwine in a sinuous Art Nouveau manner. Clusters of silver-white flowers adorn the centre-front neckline. Puffed sleeves of

spotted tulle are gathered above the elbows. Ruched lace bands over silver braid decorate the lower bodice above a silver, shaped belt. They are repeated as borders on the matching floor-length and shorter open-fronted skirts.
This young *belle* represents a physical ideal for 1905. Edwardians admired a shapely full figure and upright deportment (enforced by rigid corsetry) and were excited by a long neck and gracefully sloping shoulders.

P.101 'LOVE WHILE YOU MAY' EVENING GOWN, BODICE AND SKIRT
The bodice has a low, square décolletage edged with lace slotted with pale blue bébé ribbon, trimmed with lines of silver metallic braid and roundels of pink silk gauze roses.
The upper bodice has narrow horizontal flounces of spotted pink tulle (on a toffee-pink satin foundation) over applied rows of sparkling pink gelatin spangles. Longer tiered flounces form short sleeves.
Gathered beneath a pink belt, the matching skirt falls to a rippled hem bordered in toffee-pink satin. At thigh level it has a horizontal band of applied silver braid and roses (echoing the neckline); below are tightly packed narrow flounces and rows of spangles.
'We see *entre-deux* of lace, incrustations of pailletted embroidery, ruchings and pleatings of *mousseline de soie*, with an edging of Valenciennes lace, and these are favourite and pretty notions of trimming a simple Court or evening gown for a girl.' *The Lady's Realm*, March 1905

P.103 'THE ELUSIVE JOY OF YOUTH' EVENING GOWN, BODICE AND SKIRT
The bodice, with short puffed sleeves of spotted mauve tulle over pale pink satin, has a low neckline and is slightly pouched above a white belt. Lines of silver rickrack edge the neck, form cuffs and, with applied sparkling silver metallic floral motifs, decorate the bodice asymmetrically. Below hip-level, the trained skirt is full and adorned with horizontal rows of silver rickrack, flat silver braid and flounced tulle. Three large, graduated silver and mauve floral devices embellish the skirt's centre front.
For a 'coming-out dance' it was recommended that the angles of a girlish figure should be disguised by a bodice with ruches, frills and a slight pouch. Puffed sleeves were favoured for young women and it was vital that a petticoat had plenty of froufrou and rustle frills to swish around a débutante's feet.

P.105 'WHEN LIFE'S YOUNG PLEASURE'S WOO' EVENING GOWN, BODICE AND SKIRT
The fitted, long-fronted bodice in pale blue satin has a low, wide neckline edged with lace over pink silk and bordered with frilled gold lace over blue silk. The short sleeves have double puffs with a hint of pink roses beneath the chiffon. A roundel of artificial roses (pink

chiffon over coarse silver tissue) marks the cleavage above an *échelle* of blue bows on gold lace. This *échelle* is repeated down the matching skirt's centre-front. The skirt is smooth-line, gently eased into the waist, and has a border of mid-blue silk.

'In the evening our stays were pulled still tighter, and heavily boned satin bodices were laced over them. The décolletage was, in the case of young girls, decorously cut and a great to do was made about fitting the short sleeves decently under the arm.' Mrs C.S. Peel, *Life's Enchanted Cup*, 1933

P. 107 'INTENTION' BALL OR OPERA GOWN, BODICE AND SKIRT

The bodice (bright purple and pink satin) has a low scooped décolletage with a bertha of flounced lace over silver metallic lace. It has a bold, asymmetrical appliqué of large star-like pink flowers on one side and is threaded through with intertwined pale blue and green

velvet rouleaux on the other. The matching, trained skirt is pleated beneath a deep belt that flares out from the waist in two stiffened pleats caught by a large, ornate, gold-gilt buckle. The hem has a broad band of the applied star-like flowers and sparkling silver metal thread embroidery. With its unambiguous name, Lucile might have created this with an ambitious seductress in mind. This *femme fatale* would have needed strength and stamina to support the weighty combination of velvets, metallic embroideries and three-dimensional appliqué.

P. 109 'THE SHORTNESS OF TIME' EVENING DRESS, BODICE AND SKIRT

The bodice of lace over pink-and-white striped silk gauze with a multicoloured chiné floral pattern has a flared, plunging décolletage edged with frilled lace threaded

through with yellow ribbon. A large silver and blue butterfly-like motif marks the cleavage. Elbow-length sleeves have wide bands and cuffs of lace frills and applied silver and blue motifs. A wide cummerbund in pale blue satin is finished with a bouffant bow and long, pointed streamers reaching to the floor. The matching, slightly trained skirt is gathered into the waist and trimmed around the hem with frilled lace and rouleaux.

'Chiné *mousselines* in lovely blurred designs, melting into softly tinted backgrounds, promise to be an assured success… .' Mrs Jack May, *The Queen*, April 1904

P. 111 'MADAME ELIZABETH' DINNER GOWN, BODICE AND SKIRT

The bodice of mauve challis with a chiné pattern of small pink rosebuds has a wide scooped neckline and filmy bertha (edged with frilled lace) caught up at the centre front by a pair of red silk roses. Set in below small rectangular epaulettes, narrow, three-quarter sleeves are composed of bands of frilled lace and challis. The bodice has an elongated front

with a mauve sash tied in a bow ending in long streamers. A lace peplum covers the top of the matching, slightly trained skirt. It is tempting to speculate that this *jeune fille* gown was named after Elizabeth, the seventeen-year-old heroine in Elinor Glyn's *The Visits of Elizabeth,* 1901. The enchantingly scatty character was inspired by Lady Angela Forbes; the book's frontispiece was based on her portrait.

P. 113 'THE SWEETNESS OF LOVE' DINNER DRESS, BODICE AND SKIRT

In pale blue silk with a woven pattern of stripes and diamonds, the fitted bodice has an upper section of lace (over a spangled

chemisette) with a V neck, and a lower part of pale blue silk adorned with two large blue satin bows. Elbow-length sleeves of silk and lace ruffles are trimmed with blue satin bows. The matching, full skirt is gathered beneath a piped waist. It is one of the album's pretty, pastel-coloured gowns designed with the young and innocent in mind. Lucile was so successful with such *ingénue* creations that 'there was scarcely a fashionable mother in Town who did not bring her daughter to me to be dressed for her first season'; 'Matchmaking mothers would stare anxiously at their daughters when I had dressed them in something that showed every line of their lithe young bodies...' (*Discretions and Indiscretions*, 1932, pp.90 and 65)

P. 115 'DAPHNE' DINNER GOWN, BODICE AND SKIRT

In cream silk chiné with an all-over design of sprigs in pale pink and green, the bodice has a faux décolletage edged with a Greek

fret in salmon-pink rouleau. Similar fretwork borders the short, wide silk sleeves. The bodice is worn over a 'pneumonia' blouse with a double lace collar and sleeves of gathered lace flounces (tied with salmon pink bows) with tight lace forearms. An *échelle* of pink bows adorns the bodice front. Gathered below a bright pink belt, the minimally trained skirt is trimmed around with Greek fret rouleaux at calf-level. Representing the extremes of Edwardian style, this watercolour mannequin has an exaggerated Pompadour hair style, forward-thrust mono-bosom within a pouter pigeon bodice or kangaroo pouch, and a waist so small she is in danger of snapping in two.

'The Pompadour revival introduced in some charming silks with tiny blurred bouquets of flowers or with little sprays closely powdered over the silks.' *The Lady*, January 1905

P. 117 'REVELRY' EVENING GOWN, BODICE AND SKIRT

In pearl-white voile over gold satin, the bodice has a low, plunging décolletage edged with lace above a border of clustered pink silk rosebuds. A swathe of voile edged with gold and silver braid and embroidered with white and gold scrolling vines crosses the bodice diagonally. Matching short sleeves flare over bouffant lace under-sleeves. Below an

embroidered belt, the skirt has a V-shaped yoke into which the skirt is gathered. A wide band of embroidered fruiting vines (matching the bodice) meanders around the hem. Such sweeping froufrou skirts in combustible floating fabrics could be hazardous. At Lord Grenfell's ball in February 1905, the Duchess of Marlborough's fluffy tulle overskirt came into contact with a smouldering cigarette end and the next minute was in flames, which the gallant Lord Crichton smothered with his tunic.

P. 119 'CLIMAX' EVENING GOWN, BODICE AND SKIRT

The bodice in mid-blue silk with an overlay of chiffon has a low square décolletage

supported on blue velvet shoulder straps tied together on the neckline. The latter is trimmed with frilled cream and gold metal lace. Short sleeves of cream over gold lace flounces are attached to the shoulder straps. A blue and pink ribbon rosette and silk buds decorate the centre-front bodice. Below an ornate gold-gilt belt, the matching, softly pleated skirt has horizontal flounces and rows of ruching.

'The décolleté can be any shape, round or square or "en cœur" with shoulder straps and lower sleeves or with high puffs of tulle.' *The Lady*, June 1905

P. 121 'AN EPISODE' VISITING COSTUME, JACKET, SKIRT AND HAT

Over a lace blouse with a stand-up collar tied with a bow, and trimmed in pale blue silk and domed buttons, the tightly fitted, single-breasted jacket in dull, salmon-pink wool has revers faced with orange-pink velvet and edged with black and white braid. It fastens with two large, embroidered, tasselled, silver and white medallions. Short puffed wool

sleeves have turn-back cuffs of orange-pink velvet edged with black and white braid and silver and white embroidery (to match the medallions). Puffed, delicate under-sleeves with a lattice pattern have cuffs trimmed with small embroidered 'rococo' cartouches in pink, blue and green floss silks. Beneath a body-fitting, short, tabbed basque, the skirt is moulded over the hips and flares to a train. The black hat has a domed crown, ostrich plume and brim trimmed with a black lace ruffle.

'I have noticed that the majority of sartorial modes show a basque; it is often very short and the shortest are the smartest.' *The Lady's Realm*, December 1904

PP. 122 & 123 COSTUME FOR WALKING, TRAVELLING OR VISITING, SKIRT, JACKET, BODICE AND HAT

Over a white lace blouse with an upright collar and blue and white bow, the single-breasted jacket (of bright blue woollen cloth) has curved, piped side seams and a plastron of pale grey wool with silver soutache buttonholes and passementerie trimming. It closes above and below the plastron with silver and pale grey frogging. Wide, bracelet-length sleeves are ray-pleated into the shoulders, gathered into grey and blue cuffs

(trimmed with silver braid and black soutache) and fastened with silver frogging. A pale grey woollen belt is adorned with silver braid and fastens with a blue buckle. The trained skirt is ray-pleated at the waist; the pleats are emphasized with black soutache and tiny buttons or beads.

A matching blue bicorne hat (tilted over the brow) completes the ensemble, its crown filled with curled ostrich feathers which overflow at the back. Smart, with the right degree of showiness, this would have been perfect wear for the social convention of paying calls – the object being to keep friendships alive. The custom was governed by a strict code: the 1902 edition of the long-lived handbook *Manners and Rules of Good Society* by 'A Member of the Aristocracy' devoted twelve pages to this protocol and a further thirteen to the associated etiquette of leaving visiting cards.

Over a high-necked blouse with dainty jabot and pale blue bow, the single-breasted

bodice (of bright blue woollen cloth) fastens with gold-gilt diamond-shaped buttons. Ray pleating decorated to match the skirt fits the jacket into the high, round neck. Long gigot sleeves are gathered beneath small epaulettes and have lace ruffles slotted with pale blue ribbon at the wrists. A large, rectangular gilt buckle fastens the black belt. The skirt and bicorne hat are as above.

P. 127 WALKING OR TRAVELLING COSTUME, BODICE, SKIRT AND HAT

In bright salmon-pink wool, the fitted jacket (with concealed fastenings) has an asymmetrical cross-over front panel with a curved edge, beyond which peeps a segment of lace. A spool-shaped lace collar has a

black ribbon tie with decorated 'tassel' ends. Long, gigot sleeves are pleated beneath residual epaulettes. The matching, trained skirt is pleated below a fancy blue, gold and black belt. Shoulder heads, cuffs and skirt pleats are scattered with small, glittering beads or buttons. Perched over the brow is a tiny black and brown hat with ostrich plumes and white trim. A brown spotted veil with scrollwork hem covers the face.

'The most pronounced feature of this season's fashions is the "defined silhouette". Coats and bodices, even blouses are more or less close fitting: that is to say they follow the lines of the figure… .' *The Lady*, April 1905

P. 129 WALKING OR TRAVELLING COSTUME, JACKET, SKIRT AND HAT

Over a lace blouse with an upright collar, the single-breasted jacket has falling front panels with curved hems in sludge grey-green velvet (with a self stripe) and narrow centre-front panels of white wool trimmed with brocaded ribbon and soutache.

Wide, long sleeves are gathered into deep, turn-back white cuffs trimmed at the centre front. In black wool, the smooth, slender-line skirt falls to a long train. The small black hat with flat crown is trimmed with a swathe and cascades of black tulle and a cluster of white flowers.

A useful black skirt could be put with almost any jacket or bodice, but it had to be immaculately made. The 'new' skirt was cut close to the body and tailoring apprentices had to perfect the skill of moulding (involving steaming) the woollen cloth to obtain the correct fit.

P. 131 'FAREWELL SUMMER' VISITING GOWN, BODICE, SKIRT AND HAT

A white blouse with a stand-up collar (with silver braid ties) is trimmed with silk rosebuds and silver embroidery and worn under a two-part bodice. The upper part is of transparent brown gauze and the lower of horizontal brown lace frills and gauze ruffles. Three dark

brown ribbons tie in bows around a corselette belt. Brown frilled gauze and lace sleeves reach the elbows over bracelet-length blouse sleeves embroidered in silver. In transparent brown gauze over a pale ground, the matching, trained skirt has horizontal rows of ruched and flounced, satin-edged gauze and lace. A flattish brown hat has a crown of pleated peach-pink fabric with a silver trimming and a thrown back, spotted, scallop edged brown tulle veil. Bidding goodbye to summer's pale lace gowns, Lucile offered an autumnal version in dark brown silk machine lace (and four other types of lace) over a warm layer of matching woollen repp. Lace had long been fashion's favourite and throughout the 1890s and 1900s played a key role as a trimming or for entire garments. Mrs Aria documented its growing popularity in Autumn 1897: 'And while I am talking of lace let me chronicle the fact that it continues to be one of the gods at whose feet we worship' (*The Woman at Home*, October 1897–September 1898, p.140)

P. 133 WALKING OR VISITING COSTUME, JACKET, SKIRT AND HAT

Over a white blouse with high, turned-over collar, the fitted, single-breasted jacket in black woollen cloth and green-black velvet has ornate, vertically striped front panels in

black, white, poison-green and gold. It fastens with buttons and loops. A shaped panel at the waist is trimmed with large domed buttons of fancy gilt threads. Wide, three-quarter sleeves are eased into black, white and green striped cuffs embellished with gold braid and buttons. In black woollen cloth, the matching skirt is ray-pleated into the waist and flares to a train. Two vertical lines of sparkling soutache and domed buttons enliven the skirt's centre front. A black, bowler-like hat is trimmed with white flowers and a thrown-back voile veil. Arsenic was used in dye to obtain a pernicious shade of green in the mid-19th century, and the colour was dubbed 'poison green' – an evocative name that endured.

P. 135 WALKING COSTUME, JACKET AND SKIRT

In dusky pink woollen cloth, the short jacket has crossed-over front panels outlined in dark pink velvet. It is worn over an embroidered blouse (silver on white) with a stand-up collar and a falling lace collar, with a cascade trimmed with trailing loops of pale-blue silk ribbon. Wide, elbow-length sleeves are

gathered under dropped-shoulder lines and eased into dark pink velvet cuffs. A pair of silver and white medallions adorns the jacket above a shaped silver and pink velvet belt. In matching pink wool, the plain skirt falls to a train. Perched at a steep angle, the hat has a brim of ruched pale blue silk and a fur crown trimmed with a pair of mauve roses. Edwardian fashion columnists employed an inventive vocabulary for colours – pink, grey, brown or white were hardly sufficient. They became *vieux rose*, mouse, smoke, Quaker or stone grey, tabac brown and opal, dead or chalk white.

P. 137 'TWILIGHT AND MEMORIES' AFTERNOON GOWN, BODICE AND SKIRT

Over a delicate white blouse with high standing collar and jabot (on a green ribbon), the two-part bodice in mauve challis has an upper bolero embroidered with an ornate geometric design in braid and lace. The lower

part is straight-edged and tucks into a pointed silver corselette embroidered with silk flowers. Short sleeves with puffed shoulders have under-sleeves of flounced and ruffled lace (to the elbows) and narrow transparent voile (to the wrists). A broad, tasselled, silver tissue strap is crossed over the bust beneath a garland of pastel-coloured silk flowers. In matching challis, the softly pleated skirt flows to a long train. Mauve was a colour of half-mourning and, like grey and drab brown, had matronly overtones. 'The Baronne was dressed in pale mauve and looked lovely… .' Elinor Glyn, *The Visits of Elizabeth*, 1901 (p.192)

P. 139 'AFTERWARDS – NOTHING' EVENING GOWN, BODICE AND SKIRT

The tightly fitted bodice in black satin has a low, meandering décolletage with a chemisette of white lace edged with gold

lace. The curving neckline has infills of pale blue satin, gold lace rosettes and a central pale blue bow. Short tabbed sleeves of black satin have under-sleeves of lace gathered into ruffles by pale blue ribbons fastened with bows. A large, flared rectangular buckle emphasizes the elongated bodice. In plain black satin the box-pleated skirt terminates in a full train. Lucile derived enormous pleasure and inspiration from prints and paintings of all periods. She reworked elements from late 16th-century and early 17th-century dress in this gown, with its elongated bodice and slashed sleeves. Undisciplined borrowing from historical styles was common in Edwardian dress design: '…we seem determined to ignore any given rules, and mingle the modes of the Directoire and 1830, the Victorian and the François Premier. With a Directoire coat you see a Marie Antoinette hat.' (*The Queen*, October 1904)

P. 143 OPERA COAT

In bronze silk taffeta the voluminous *saque* garment has panels that flare to a wide, knee-length hem. A high-waisted white dicky is decorated with gold metallic lace and has applied lines of purple-pink shadow grosgrain ribbon. The garment is trimmed around the neck, front edges and over-seams with lines

of rouleaux and ruched bands of silk taffeta. Two long gold ties with tasselled ends hang from the neck. Side panels have rouleau scrollwork. Capacious sleeves with deep flared cuffs are set into dropped shoulders. Gold metallic lace motifs trim shoulder heads, cuffs and side panels. It is worn over a black skirt with a long train.

A lavish opera coat, cloak or wrap often doubled as *sortie de bal*. Opera performances (especially first nights) at Covent Garden were highlights of the Edwardian Season, and society women vied with each other to appear in the most magnificent creation of the evening.

P. 145 'BECAUSE' EVENING GOWN, BODICE AND SKIRT

The bodice, in green satin with an overlay of green silk mesh, has a plunging, lace-edged décolletage with embroidered (in yellow or gold threads) borders that curve over the

shoulders and down the centre front. A *bouquet de corsage* in pale blue (to match a narrow belt) adorns the neckline. Matching short sleeves flare above ruffled lace under-sleeves. A trained, green satin skirt has a mesh over-skirt with embroidered borders and handkerchief points. A curvaceous blonde displays the gown – perhaps Lucile agreed with fashion journalist Mrs Eric Pritchard: 'Green is rather popular now for evening wear; there are so many shades of it that you may find one to suit you. But, as I have said before, green for day or evening wear is a colour for fair people only.' (*The Lady's Realm*, November 1903)

P. 149 'ENRAPTURE' BALL OR OPERA GOWN, BODICE AND SKIRT

In burnt-rose silk taffeta, the swathed, fitted bodice has a low scooped, off-the-shoulder neckline with a lace camisole, a bertha embroidered with pink-silver tissue roses and under-sleeves of layered lace frills. A shaped belt in pink-brown velvet has faux cross-lacing in pink velvet rouleaux. The skirt is softly pleated at the waist and finishes in a long train. A lavishly long lace flounce bordered with gold lace is caught by garlands of artificial flowers at knee level. A ruched band of pink velvet circles the skirt a few inches above the hem. A silver leaf spray ornament is pinned into the hair.
'Ball dresses are as ethereal and fragile as we can well make them. Lace, tulle, chiffon and flowers enter into their composition. They 'droop' considerably off the shoulders and curl off into long, narrow trains.' *The Woman at Home*, April–September 1901 (p.553)

P. 151 'OBLIVION' EVENING GOWN, BODICE AND SKIRT

In black spotted tulle (scattered with black sequins) over a bright blue ground, the bodice has a plunging neckline trimmed with lace and is embellished with large black appliqué flowers enclosing a purple bow at the

cleavage. Puffed, short sleeves (set over pink silk and trimmed with appliqué flowers) are gathered into frilled cuffs. Below a shaped blue corselette, the skirt has a panel of artificial flowers and is decorated with bands and a border of black diamond mesh. A purple silk petticoat can be glimpsed below the hemline. The name suggests loss, and it is possible that this sombre-hued gown was intended for half-mourning after the unrelenting black of full mourning was discarded. Mourning was still rigorously observed, and Lucile boasted of 'Consolable Sorrow', a Lucile gown in deepest black that (according to her) every widow in London purchased.

P. 152 PEIGNOIR

In fine pink woollen gauze, the loose, calf-length 'at home' garment is in the *saque* style with a V neck above an elaborate gold passementerie fastening. The front panels (bordered with gold braid and pink silk

flowers) sit edge-to-edge. Tiny pin tucks contain the fullness over the shoulders and long, ample, draped sleeves are set into dropped shoulder lines. Wide, open cuffs are bordered with gold lace and pink silk flowers, and lined with rows of lace frills decorated with delicate pink ribbon rosebuds on green cord stems. The garment is edged throughout with fur and worn over a trained skirt in a black lightweight spotted fabric. '…lovely Mrs Bovill who had been the 'Beauty' of that year's London Season. I was thrilled by her beautiful pink satin peignoir and quilted slippers and longed most ardently to become a Society lady just like her.' Elinor Glyn, *Romantic Adventure*, 1936 (p.16)

P. 153 'UNFORGOTTEN' EVENING GOWN, BODICE AND SKIRT

In mauve, fancy-weave silk, the bodice has a low décolletage edged with frilled lace above peach and orange silk velvet and silver braid. Over the bust, the fine silk is gathered into a circular motif decorated with sequinned pendants. Short sleeves with turned-back cuffs have elbow-length under-sleeves of lace frills trimmed with silver braid. A shaped belt in peach and orange silk velvet echoes the neckline border. With spaced

pleating at the waist, the matching silk skirt has a short train and purple border.

Although deodorants had been available since the mid-1880s, many varieties of underarm dress preservers, protectors or shields were used to stop perspiration ruining precious silks in hot ball rooms. Adding yet another component to the paraphernalia of Edwardian under-pinnings, they were considered necessary additions to one's gown.

P. 154 WALKING COSTUME, JACKET, SKIRT AND HAT
The short, *saque* jacket of dark brown woollen plush and brown wool is edge-to-edge fastened with three long, decorated clasps. The front panels are enclosed by lines of

scalloped braid. A bow at the neck in silver tissue on white wool with gold braid trimming has a curved stole with applied floral motifs. The three-quarter sleeves are wide and flared. A plain black skirt (with train) is finely pleated beneath a shaped belt with a large oval gold gilt buckle. A small black hat has a flat crown and is trimmed with a swathe of tulle and a cluster of white flowers.
'Walking about the London streets trailing clouds of dust was horrid. I once found I had carried into the house a banana skin which had got caught up in the unstitched hem of my dress.' Lady Cynthia Asquith, *Remember and be Glad*, 1952 (p.77)

P. 156 WALKING COSTUME, BODICE, SKIRT AND HAT
Over a blouse with a stand-up neck and black bow trim, the short *saque* jacket in mottled grey and black long-haired plush has edge-to-edge fastening with scalloped fancy borders. Wrist-length, wide bishop sleeves are gathered into the shoulders and into

deep cuffs. An ermine stole is crossed over the centre front. Front panels and cuffs are decorated with frogged motifs. A simple black skirt flares to a short train. A grey hat has a domed crown with green silk band (threaded through a gilt buckle) and curved brim edged with purple and trimmed with a circle of predominantly mauve flowers. Ermine, with its royal associations, was expensive and apart from modest tippets, stoles and hidden linings, was considered inappropriate for day wear. It became dirty very quickly but could be cleaned with liberal quantities of cornflour.

P. 157 EVENING GOWN, BODICE AND SKIRT
In eye-catching shimmering gold metallic fabrics and taffeta trimmed with sequinned clusters, the bodice has a low, square neckline edged with rippled lace and bordered with green, white and gold embroidery. It has short

sleeves of tulle flounces. A purple *bouquet de corsage* adorns the neck. The skirt is trained and its diaphanous spangled tulle overskirt is open along the centre front and bordered

with an ornate, three-dimensional floral design in white and gold.
Each tiny watercolour mannequin in the album has been painted with infinite care and given its own character, hair colour and make-up.
Here a cupid's bow mouth is blood-red, the cheeks are rouged and big eyes darkened. Late 1890s and 1900s magazines gave advice on make-up but discretion was the watchword, and *maquillage* had to be done in the privacy of one's boudoir.

P. 158 WALKING OR TRAVELLING COSTUME, BODICE, SKIRT AND HAT
In black plush, the short jacket has a cross-over front fastened with an elaborate trellised bow motif, and is cut away to reveal a lace blouse. Lines of intertwined soutache trim the fronts. A short ermine tie is fastened

around the high neck with a small trellised bow. Wide sleeves are gathered into the shoulders and into bracelet-length, ermine-trimmed cuffs. The trained skirt is pleated at the waist under a shaped black belt and descends to a train. The small black hat has a flat crown and is trimmed with a swathe of tulle and a cluster of white flowers. A detail at top left illustrates the jacket when it is open – its revers are faced with lace-edged voile.

P. 159 'L'ALLEGRO' EVENING GOWN, BODICE AND SKIRT
The bodice, in swathed toffee-pink chiffon over ecru satin, has a low neckline with an embroidered edging in pink and gold. Below is an asymmetrical arrangement of a silvered sash crossed by lacing in bright and pale pink

velvet caught by domed 'buttons' and ending in decorative pendants. Bold star flowers in gold and almost fluorescent pink metal strip adorn the bodice and shoulders. Short sleeves of tulle and chiffon puff over the tops of long white kid gloves. The matching, trained skirt is decorated with shimmering star flowers and has three horizontal tucks above the hem.
When designing a gown to be seen from a distance at a large function, Lucile selected bright colours and glittering, large scale embroideries. She claimed that the effect was instantaneous and made people exclaim 'Oh!'. ('The Evolution of a Dress', *New York American Examiner*, 1910)

P. 160 DINNER GOWN, BODICE AND SKIRT
Above a lace chemisette bordered with pale pink chiffon rosebuds, the bodice of diaphanous, pale blue fine silk, edged with white and silver gimp, is crossed over and very slightly pouched into a silver and pale blue shaped belt. Puffed sleeves are swathed about the arm-tops and gathered at the elbows by

pale blue ribbon with bows. The matching, trained skirt is plain with a spotted tulle streamer adorning the back. This 'quiet gown', a demure creation, complied with Lucile's principle that a dress for a small room and intimate occasion had to be subtle and without 'repellent embroideries' or 'hard glittering jewellery' (*The New York American Examiner*, 1910).

P. 162 EVENING GOWN, BODICE AND SKIRT
In pearl-white silk, the fitted bodice (over a camisole of lace slotted with pale blue bébé ribbon) has a low scooped neckline bordered

with pale blue beneath a transparent fichu with frilled edges pinned at the cleavage with a single pink rose. Bands of pale blue silk are criss-crossed over the bodice, pass around the waist and fall in two fringed streamers to knee level. Narrow, gauged three-quarter sleeves have frilled cuffs tied with pale blue bows. The skirt is ruched into the waist and is very slightly trained.
'Well, to tell you about the ball. First my white tulle was a dream. Octavia said it was by far the prettiest debutante frock she had ever seen.' Elinor Glyn, *The Visits of Elizabeth*, 1901 (p.270)

P. 163 WALKING COSTUME, JACKET, SKIRT AND HAT
Over a blouse with a high, bow trimmed standing collar, the short jacket in brown fur has a curved 'yoke' and is cut to a point at the front. White revers are embroidered with

fancy linear motifs in metal soutache and braid, and a white gilet is decorated with gold braid and a double lace cascade. Wide sleeves are constructed in one with the front panels, and eased into ruffled lace cuffs trimmed with gold braid. The black cloth skirt has top-stitched pleats and falls to a long train. The small black hat has a flat crown and is trimmed with a cluster of white flowers while a swathe of tulle cascades at the back.

P. 164 COSTUME, COAT, SKIRT AND HAT
Over a blouse with an upright collar and black bow tie, the seven-eighths coat in black woollen cloth is tightly fitted and has long black revers flanking panels of white

wool fastened with 'military' gold braid and buttons. The top is caped over wrist-length narrow sleeves. Turned-back cuffs and cape are trimmed with buttoned tabs in silver metal thread.
The coat's gored lower panels are eased into a scalloped waist seam, mould the hips closely and are open along the centre front. The matching, plain skirt has a train. A grey-purple hat has a domed crown with a green silk band (threaded through a gilt buckle) and a purple-edged, curved brim

trimmed with a circle of predominantly mauve flowers.
'Hats were monuments of tulle or lace, trimmed with bouquets of plumes or else regular herbaceous borders… .' V.C. Sermoneta, *Things Past*, 1929 (p.93)

P. 165 'THE MOMENT' EVENING GOWN, BODICE AND SKIRT
The album concludes on a strong note – a powerful gown in purple and bright blue satin with blue chiffon. The bodice has a low

décolletage edged with lace and a central three-dimensional arrangement in swathed chiffon which resembles the prow of a ship. This extraordinary feature rises above an ornate border of gold lace, while arranged

alongside is a *bouquet de corsage* of purple-blue pom-pom flower heads. Short puffed purple sleeves have cuffs with streamers in blue chiffon. Over a purple foundation the blue chiffon skirt has seams and hem bordered with a Greek fret in white braid and gold lace. The seams are partially slit to reveal a vivid purple petticoat beneath – prefiguring the leg-revealing, slashed side skirts that became familiar and tantalizing features of Lucile gowns in the years before World War I.

'Carresaute', an Evening Gown

'Lucile worked with soft materials, delicately springling [sic] them with bead or sequin embroidery, with cobweb lace insertions, true lovers' knots, and garlands of minute roses. Her colour sense was so subtle that the delicacy of detail could scarcely be seen at a distance, though the effect she created was of an indefinable shimmer.'

Cecil Beaton[1]

It was an extraordinary coincidence that, at the time of writing, the evening dress 'Carresaute', depicted in Lucile's Autumn 1905 album, should be offered for sale, spotted and purchased by the V&A. It had originally belonged to a Norwegian opera singer and was preserved by her family until the 1960s, when it became part of a private costume collection.[2] Few early Lucile garments survive, so this particular dress provides us with a rare opportunity to compare the actual garment with its painted depiction.

The album's lively watercolours and pasted-in fabrics are almost as fresh as the day they were put in, but the gown itself is no longer pristine, having endured over a hundred years of being handled, packed and displayed. It is missing the centre-front *bouquet de corsage* of three full-blown pink rose heads – Lucile would have designed this as a focal point but, being an external feature, it was simple to remove or replace. Such silk flowers were extremely delicate and often suffered, quickly becoming droopy and 'tired'. The trailing, sparkling-white and silver tissue sash, with its oval buckle and tasselled ends, has also vanished. Often accessories such as this were used on other gowns and, being relatively small, were easily lost (although it might have tarnished badly and been discarded). The artist painted a minuscule waist in accordance with the prevailing mode, but as the photograph of the actual gown reveals, its opera singer owner (even when corseted) had a 'normal' waist measurement. Otherwise the water-colour and ensemble are remarkably close companions: the style – short sleeves, pouched bodice and slightly trained skirt – as well as the details – the number of flounces, disposition of laces and embroidery, tiny rosebuds nestling around the neckline – match almost exactly.

Mid-blue and turquoise fabrics featured extensively in Lucile's Autumn 1905 collection – it is the colour of the ensemble selected for the first page. Lucile described colour as her religion. She wrote: 'Blue stands for purity, for love, too, but for a very different love from that of purple; blue is for homely love, and peaceful, happy things. It is a colour all men love… .'[3] It is not surprising that she incorporated this colour in her interiors. In 1917, when she was living in New York, Lucile told the readers of *Harper's Bazaar*, 'I enter my home through a large hall that is a vivid turquoise green, with every bit of furniture and hangings and carpet, the same hue; the ceiling is vivid blue. These colours stand for success and loyalty.'[4] For fashionable dress, exquisite shades of blue were constants:

in 1921 American *Vogue* wrote, 'Lucile reserves a special corner of her sumptuous palette for the many shades of blue which she loves and which she combines with such audacity.'[5]

'Carresaute' comprises a bodice and skirt, which was entirely typical at this time: it is the complexity of make, decorative devices and subtly shifting palette that render it so distinctly 'Lucile'. Apart from the silk taffeta foundation, the dress is hand-stitched. The bodice is cut horizontally to encircle the body without the use of side seams, while the exterior is made from vertical, shirred bands of pale turquoise silk chiffon, which has been pouched into a scallop-edged ribbon running along the décolletage. The chiffon is decorated with two bands of eau-de-nil lace, one longer than the other. Beneath the chiffon lies a double layer of swathed ecru lace, onto which a meandering pale-green silk ribbon with tiny, pink silk rosebuds has been applied. Under this a layer of cream silk is decorated with green and silver metal strip embroidery in a foliate design applied to a tulle base. The lining is made of pale peach silk taffeta, which is overlaid with a short facing.

Short sleeves feature decorative tiered flounces: the one at the top is shirred and the second is gathered and seamed centrally, to form a double-layered band. The middle layer comprises accordion-pleated eau-de-nil silk chiffon with a border of shearing and rosebud rouleaux. The under-sleeves are made from ecru tape lace, which has a meandering patterned edge and extends to form the cuffs. The internal foundation is firmly boned (nine bones, within silk twill bone channels, arranged in clusters of three). At the mid-point of the plunging décolletage is a hidden interior decorative silk bow, while a fine silk ribbon drawstring is laced along the inner neckline to permit tightening. Neckline and waistband are bound with a top-mounted silk tape. A heavy cream-coloured silk grosgrain waist stay has 'Lucile Ltd, 23 Hanover Sq London W.' woven in bright, mid-

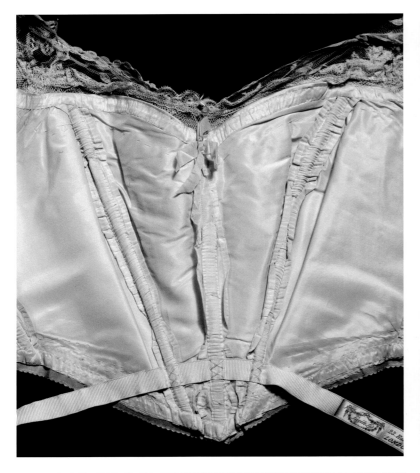

green silk. Each branch of Lucile Ltd had an individual dress label with its own address woven into it.

The internal hand-stitching is quite crude and reveals that the bodice was taken in, probably during a client fitting. It fastens at the centre back with metal hooks and eyes. A single silk-bound circle remains on the waistline, one of many that would have been attached (by hooks) to the skirt, holding it in position.

The long skirt has horizontal flounces (like the sleeves), which are composed of lace, shirring, silk chiffon and flounces. A single band of metal strip embroidery matches that on the bodice. The foundation is made from a dark-cream silk satin duchesse with ecru lace and silver-gilt lace along the centre. Around the hemline is a deep facing of cream-coloured plain weave silk with a flat, gathered ruffle mounted with a 'rustle frill' of pinked and scalloped paper taffeta, intended to make an alluring, rustling sound when the wearer moved. In Elinor Glyn's *The Visits of Elizabeth* (1901), the heroine described two distant relatives: 'They looked very well bred and respectable, and badly dressed; nothing rustled nicely when they walked.' The swishing noise of layered silk underskirts was an important (seductive) feature of early 1900s dress – the French for 'rustle' is '*froufrou*', a word now synonymous with the elaborate confections of frills, ruches and flounces so crucial to Edwardian gowns.

"Carresaute".

Chapter Three '...the raiment of allurement...' 1906–1935

Postcard of the actress Lily Elsie as Sonia in *The Merry Widow* (1907), wearing the famous 'immense black crinoline hat'. *The Play Pictorial* (vol. X, no. 61) was fulsome in its praise for Lucile's costumes for Lily Elsie: 'In the first act she is gowned in what appears to be woven sunshine but is in reality a shimmer of silver and gold embroideries over oyster-white satin.' Foulsham and Banfield

'... the raiment of allurement...' [1]

1906–1914

TOP Pencil sketch of a walking or visiting costume, 1907–8. A high-waisted skirt has a slender profile and graceful train, and is decorated with a snaking band (a motif used in 1905: see page 59). Over a pouched blouse, the slightly flared jacket, trimmed with buttons and *galon*, is cropped short to exaggerate the skirt's long lines. In *Merry Widow* mode, ostrich feathers adorn the large picture hat.

BOTTOM Pencil sketch of a day ensemble, 1907–8. Over what appears to be a one-piece, long-sleeved dress, a short-sleeved, open-fronted bolero is caught together just below the bust. Supple, plain fabric adds impact to long, sweeping lines, although, with her love of decoration, Lucile could not resist finishing the skirt with a panel of geometric embroidery. Wide-brimmed hats became repositories for a multitude of fancy work; in this case the crown is obscured by hand-crafted flowers.

Considering Lucile's achievements between the early 1900s and 1913, Cecil Beaton eulogized: 'Never, surely, has the dressmaker's art soared to such heights as in the dresses of this period designed by that delicate genius, Lucille [*sic*]'.[2] Yet the majestic curves and sweeping hems of the high Edwardian silhouette (as portrayed in the 1905 album) were destined for extinction. The mechanics of anchoring a bodice and skirt together around the waist with 'quite un-get-able-at intricacies of hooks and eyes'[3] concealed by a deep, boned belt, were frustrating. It was crucial to keep the garments together to maintain 'the set' of an ensemble, not an easy task; to stop a skirt sagging at the back an additional 'ornamented safety pin could be stuck through the belt'.[4] Since the 1890s women could escape these exasperating problems in one-piece Directoire tea gowns and dresses cut *en princesse,* and it was the streamlined structure and relative simplicity of such attire that was to prevail. Preliminary pencil sketches for a Lucile collection of 1907–8 capture a transitional moment in the evolution of the high-waisted, one-piece gown. Skirts remain long and trained but bodices have svelte contours while cropped jackets emphasize the elongated lines. High-waisted gowns in pliant fabrics had floating overskirts, soon to be major features in the Lucile repertoire (*see opposite, top; overleaf, top and bottom*). Corset construction was adapted to achieve modish, stretched-out curves, and corsetry with complementary dainty lingerie in a tempting range of colours was available at 23 Hanover Square.

As a young man Cecil Beaton was entranced with the mystique of the stars of light opera, and they, especially Lily Elsie, became his lifelong heroines. With his innate understanding of fashion he pinpointed the synergy between these glorious creatures and the equally gorgeous gowns designed for them on and off stage by Lucile. It was a natural progression for Lucile to move from dressing amateur theatricals and *tableaux vivants* to costuming professional productions in the later 1890s. Her contact with the stage and its players had a unique offshoot: Lucile fashion shows. These personal theatres of fashion were played out beneath scaled-down proscenium arches. In June 1908, *The Illustrated London News* commented: 'At Mme Lucile's in Hanover Square, there is a charming little theatre where clients of the house assemble to see the latest novelties.' After posing on stage the mannequins descended to walk about among the audience. Emulating theatre programmes, leaflets were printed with the running order of her fashion parades. They reveal the Lucile range, from tailored coats and skirts, smart afternoon ensembles and cloth dresses, to summery voiles and muslins, Ascot dresses and ubiquitous tea gowns. Seventy-two ensembles are listed in a programme for May 1906 and 51 for the February 1909 show. These two occasions appear not to be as ambitious as the 1904 'Curves and Colours' private view, with its thematic *mise-en-scènes* and musical accompaniment, or the 1905 'The Seven Ages of Woman' parade, patronized by Princess Margaret, 'Daisy', of Connaught, then in the process of acquiring her Lucile trousseau. In her autobiography, Lucile recollected this particular 'rites of passage' fashion show with obvious pride.

Lucile's claim to have almost single-handedly banished ponderous costume from the stage has to

LEFT A Lucile mannequin in day wear, London, c. 1906. A sideways pose captures the shapely figure in a cloth gown with train, cross-over bodice, winged shoulders and elaborate sleeves. Favourite themes, colour combinations and trimmings recur throughout Lucile's *oeuvre*. She had a penchant for fur bands, as seen here, bordering sleeves and skirt.

be put in perspective. Society, fashion and theatre magazines of the early 1900s indicate that the shift from weighty to lighter stage attire was already a general phenomenon in London, while in Paris couturiers – notably Worth, Paquin and Doucet – were dressing famous actresses in gossamer fabrics. Kaplan and Stowell's erudite investigations illuminate the significant role Lucile played in this on-stage fashion shift.[5] Play after play featured leading ladies in a sequence of the latest styles while journalists, as if attending a fashion show, described each ensemble with precision – the dramatic content seemed immaterial. In productions with contemporary plots (some taken from the world of fashion), theatrical costume was virtually synonymous with fashionable dress – in February 1910, *The Play Pictorial* recorded: 'nowhere are more lovely or more fashionable frocks to be seen than on the stage of our West End theatres'. Lucile's standards were just as exacting for the theatre as they were for her private clients – the gowns were constructed with infinite care and meticulous attention to detail, rather than hurriedly assembled with inferior materials solely for dramatic impact. Indeed, Beaton described them as 'masterpieces of intricate workmanship'.[6] A sketchbook compiled by Lucile in the summer of 1904 (during a stay with Elsie de Wolfe and companions at Le Petit Trianon, Versailles) has preliminary ideas for Seymour Hicks' *The Catch of the Season*, which opened at London's Vaudeville Theatre in September that year. The sketches, though unfinished, are accomplished and bear comparison with images of fashionable and sensual Edwardian girls by the graphic artists Charles Dana Gibson and Harry Furniss. Acknowledging that a play's success often depended upon the approval of women in the audience who were seduced by modish costumes, impresarios went to Lucile for 'gowns *de luxe*' in 'wondrous colours and entrancing forms'.[7] Never one to miss an opportunity for publicity, Lucile held a private view of her contributions to *The Catch of the Season* at La Salle Lucile five days before the first night. The production marked the debut of the Gibson Girls, a much-photographed chorus line of actresses, hailed as 'very striking, their dresses being many and varied'.[8] Each frothy gown was different and all were intricately decorated – they would not have looked out of place in an elegant drawing room.

Fashion display was a vital element at all levels of the fashion business, whether static in shop windows, or animated on a 'living model' in the rarefied ambiance of a designer's salon. Lucile's particular talents for showmanship resulted in key developments in the art of fashion presentation and significant advances in the evolution of the mannequin's role. French art historian Arsène Alexandre's illuminating 1902 discourse on mannequins compared them to actresses and the fashion salon to a theatre – ideas completely in tune with Lucile's philosophy.[9] Initially, she selected six attractive young girls who could interpret the Lucile look under her direction either in fashion parades or in intimate presentations to clients. She always took pride in her mannequins and was an admirable mentor; she made sure her charges ate properly; took them to art galleries; encouraged them to empathize with all that the House of Lucile signified; and was genuinely delighted if they married well. Rare photographs of Lucile ensembles 1904–5 capture somewhat diffident Edwardian mannequins in elaborate confections posed against painted bosky or plain backdrops. By 1912, under Lucile's firm tutelage, they were transformed into ultra-assured figures gliding in the calm of her salon or posing elegantly in her Paris town garden (*top*). According to her autobiography, in 1907 Lucile assumed a Svengali-like role when she groomed a less-than-confident Lily Elsie for her lead in Franz Lehár's *The Merry Widow*. The operetta was an instant success and Lily Elsie in Lucile costumes secured celebrity status for herself and acclaim for the House of Lucile. Postcards disseminated images of Lily Elsie in her shimmering, layered tubular gowns and celebrated *Merry Widow* hat: the hat, 'which I designed

TOP The languid mannequin Dolores in a Directoire summer afternoon gown in the garden at rue de Penthièvre, Paris, 1912. A silk charmeuse underdress beneath a high-waisted tunic of chiffon fits seductively close to the body, while a narrow train with a decorative border trails on the gravel path. A parasol, broad-brimmed hat and long white gloves deflect the sun's rays. Photograph: Henri Manuel

BOTTOM Lily Elsie in her wedding gown, 8 November 1911. In the prevailing high-waisted Empire style, beneath a trained overdress of white ninon and stamped velvet with ermine borders, the dress had a V-necked chiffon bodice and layered skirt embellished with seed pearls and bugle beads, while a pearl-strewn sash of silver tissue had streamers finished with beaded fringes to match the skirt's scalloped hemline. Photographed against a fussy backdrop of door grills, draped chintz curtains and aspidistra fronds, the gown has lost some of its impact. *The Times of India*, 27 November 1911. Photograph: Foulsham and Banfield

for Lily Elsie brought in a fashion which carried the name of "Lucile" its creator all over Europe and the States'.[10] Indeed, the black picture hat (made in Paris to a Lucile design?) with its silver band and pink roses tucked under the brim, started a profitable craze for Lucile and copyists. Years later, over lunch with Cecil Beaton in summer 1941, Lily Elsie was to remark: 'But I never understood why that black hat I wore in the last act was such a sensation. It arrived from Paris a few days before we opened. It had a few black wisps of paradise on it; it wasn't particularly large but created a craze for huge hats. It became the Merry Widow hat.'[11]

In the years before World War I, line drawings by Lucile's in-house fashion artists were invariably based on Lily Elsie's iconic poise and beauty. She considered that everything Lucile made was a work of art and after wearing these clothes could not go to another designer. Lucile went on to design many of this actress's theatre costumes and off-stage clothes (*see page 183; previous page, bottom*). Inscribed sketches indicate the individual attention that she accorded Lily Elsie (*see page 210*) and in 1911, for her marriage to Major Ian Bullough, the actress commissioned her wedding gown and trousseau from Lucile. The white wedding gown was judged to be perfect for a winter ceremony (*see page 185*). To keep crowds away, the marriage had not been announced so there were few to marvel at the filmy, pearl-studded whiteness of the dress, through which could be glimpsed 'a fascinating suggestion of the flesh pink ninon and charmeuse of the under robe' (*The Times of India*, November 1911). Lavish and extensive, the trousseau had chemises, nightdresses, tea gowns and petticoats, mainly in pale pink silks and satins trimmed with pink, lilac or blue rouleaux, tiny ribbon flowers and lace. Up to half a dozen versions of favourite ensembles were made in different colours and fabrics and, most extravagantly, nine copies of a simple coat and skirt costume dubbed 'The Curate' were ordered. Seductive evening gowns included 'a mere cloud of dawn pink and white chiffon, with traces of milky pearls and a wonderfully draped creation of black chiffon velvet which fastens invisibly somewhere across the back, and in the front is so caught up and slit open to give a full and fascinating view of an ankle and foot clad in flesh pink silk...'.[12] For added allure, the latter had a fish-tail train with a daring, vivid purple satin lining. Because both theatre costume and fashion with the Lucile label shared careful design, and precise cut and construction, it is often difficult to distinguish one from the other. A few sketches made between 1909 and 1912 are marked 'specials' and were clearly exclusive to theatrical productions while very similar designs were duplicated to be sent out to customers as part of seasonal collections. Lily Elsie dedicated her Christmas and New Year greetings, 1912–13, to Lucile over a photograph of herself wearing an evening gown (*top*: Lily's real name was Elsie Bullough). The gown was a model available to any Lucile client. For Lily Elsie, the gown was amended so that the sash tied at the right and a beaded swag no longer adorned the bodice.

In 1907 Lucile and Elinor were both in New York where *The New York Times* recorded their sightseeing activities; reporters pressed them for interviews and they were lionized by members of the Four Hundred (the elite of New York society). Elinor's trip resulted in the entertaining picaresque, *Elizabeth Visits America* (1909), while Lucile consolidated her plans for a New York branch of Lucile Ltd. Visiting the city two years later in the company of interior decorator Elsie de Wolfe, Lucile was encouraged further, taking a lease on a house near Fifth Avenue before returning to London. By February 1910 she was back with a collection of gowns and four mannequins (Gamela, Corisande, Florence and Phyllis) to launch Lucile, New York – although in doing so she began a business tangle that was eventually to have dire consequences. Making much of her English title and aristocratic clientele, an agent publicized the arrival of Lucile Ltd, and the enterprising Lady Duff Gordon fed New York's

TOP Lily Elsie's Christmas greetings to Lucile, written on a photograph of her in a Lucile evening gown: 'for Xmas and 1913'. This portrait, together with two others in the same gown (one with a fur coat), were published by J. Beagles & Co. Reproduced in *Discretions and Indiscretions*, 1932

BOTTOM Print of a Lucile evening gown of embroidered tulle, chiffon and charmeuse with a broad velvet cummerbund and sash, 1912. Clients would consider a design in the privacy of their own home and then the garment could be ordered and made to measure – an up-market retailing method that borrowed elements from shopping by post. These cards were usually inscribed with a returns warning on the back. It is indicative of Lucile's disinterest in financial affairs that in the early 1900s the fine levied for non-return of a print was 7s.6d.: it was still 7s.6d in the 1920s.

perennial desire 'to be amused, thrilled and surprised all at the same time'.[13] American hospitality, verve and wealth fuelled her ambition. She was astounded at the prices rich women were prepared to pay for clothes and happy to beguile them with her elaborate creations and fashion parades. Shrewd analysis of the American attitude towards dress and money was employed to promote sales and with typical immodesty Lucile announced: 'I became the rage,'[14] listing Mrs Reginald Vanderbilt, Mrs Stuyvesant Fish and Mrs Payne Whitney among her prestigious and affluent clients. Their husbands' immense fortunes came from railroads, shipping, banking and innumerable other business interests. Like her sister, Lucile admired the well-dressed American's 'perfect and soignée appearance'[15] and for a dozen years she provided them with enchanting collections bearing her distinctive hallmarks.

In April 1911, once again encouraged by friends and with her customary enthusiasm and energy, Lady Duff Gordon inaugurated her Paris branch at rue de Penthièvre with a fashion parade of her latest collection shown to the strains of an unseen orchestra. Her autobiography makes much of the stereotypical Parisian antipathy to English fashion designers but asserts that she conquered Paris with creative collections, signature fashion parades and innovations. The opening was a resounding success '…it must be confessed that "Lucille" [sic] has attracted a bigger crowd this week in Paris than any other individual.'[16] Intrepid as ever, she declared herself responsible for various fashion revolutions – to be the first to abandon upright, boned collars; to have triumphantly introduced the 'Peter Pan neck' as well as the 'Quaker Girl' collar, and to have launched a vogue for coloured wigs. There is no doubt that she promoted round necks, without stand-up collars; used curve-edged collars that took their name from J.M. Barrie's *Peter Pan* (premiered in December 1904), and favoured demure day dresses with falling collars (Lucile designed costumes for Gertie Millar in *The Quaker Girl*, 1910). *The Illustrated London News*, November 1913, devoted a double-page colour spread to a group of Lucile ensembles teamed to dramatic effect with wigs of 'somewhat bizarre colourations [sic]' (green, blue, red and purple). Lucile habitués were accustomed to wigs – they were second nature to actresses, while her society clients wore them for *tableaux vivants*, amateur theatricals, fancy-dress balls and *bals poudrés*. It was but a short and amusing step to wear them in vivid colours to enhance one's latest Lucile tango frock.

Destined to become a top couturier, Edward Molyneux started his career in fashion providing sketches for Lucile Ltd around 1910 when he was 19 years old. A slender Molyneux sketchbook includes annotated designs signed by him (*top*) while other works by his hand are located on single sheets in the Archive. His sketches reveal a light touch, and notes in what appears to be his sloping writing show his mastery of fabrics and garment construction. Lucile recognized his considerable ability and encouraged this 'pale, delicate boy'.[17] He soon graduated from sketching the models she designed to creating originals for Lucile Ltd. Present in this volume is a tantalizingly faint pencil outline of a high-waisted Directoire dress inscribed (probably in Lucile's hand): 'red Poiret model we bought from Debenham & Freebody' (*centre*). It seems to be Paul Poiret's 'Pompon', a long tunic in red muslin scattered with red, white and green flowers over a blue silk velvet sheath dress, or possibly the almost identical 'Isadora', both dated 1910–11.[18] Keeping a watchful eye on the competition was and remains regular practice in the fashion industry. Occasionally (as in this case), examples of a rival's work are acquired for 'inspiration'. A second fleeting line drawing implies that the red Poiret was at the root of a Lucile stage costume for Lily Elsie. Lucile and Paul Poiret (16 years younger) followed parallel fashion trajectories and their autobiographies, published in 1932 and 1931 respectively, have remarkably similar self-laudatory overtones. Though keenly aware of each other's oeuvre and its

TOP Watercolour design for a black satin ensemble by Edward Molyneux, 1912. In sloping hand-writing, the description reads 'a black satin coat and skirt, the coat with one rever only on left side, caught round waist with black satin and large lover's knot of satin. The coat turned back at sides and held in place with a wreathtulle [sic] of black tulle roses. Short skirt, round knees is a band of satin with a true lover's knot and a wreath of black tulle roses coat and sleeve in one.'

CENTRE Swift pencil sketch (either by Edward Molyneux or Lucile) of a Paul Poiret gown ('Pompon' or 'Isadora'), 1911–12, purchased from Debenham & Freebody. A few faint lines captured the essence of the Paris gown. Its acquisition by Lucile Ltd reveals that Lucile secretly esteemed the work of Poiret, one of her greatest rivals.

BOTTOM Postcard of the actress Gabrielle Ray (1883–1973) dressed for the part of Daisy in Willner and Grünbaum's *The Dollar Princess*, 1909. The delicate Empire-style gown has a short-sleeved, open-fronted tunic in striped gauze over a gown with a deep border of meandering bands of ruched lace interspersed with clusters of silk flowers. A full-blown rose adorns the V-neck. Miss Ray lifts the gown to reveal a typical lace-edged, beribboned Lucile petticoat and her almond-toed satin tango pumps. Photograph: Bassano

place in fashion's continuum, they avoid even a brief mention of each other. As fashion and social historian Alison Adburgham concluded: 'They must have been deadly rivals. After all, Lucile invaded Paris: both of them were egotistic, vain and temperamental.'[19]

From time to time Molyneux joined Lucile in Paris and New York; surviving designs indicate their close working relationship, with some having both signatures and others being Molyneux trials for final versions approved and signed 'Lucile'. She gave him due praise: 'Molyneux was especially successful in designing for the stage, for, like all very young designers, he had at that time a craze for the bizarre and exotic, nothing was too vivid for him, nothing too extravagant.'[20] In the heady years before the outbreak of World War I, Paris clientele included leading vaudeville stars and fashionable courtesans (often the roles were twinned) – the likes of Gaby Deslys, La Belle Otero and Mata Hari. Lucile's ultimate reward was to see her designs worn by outstanding beauties. On occasion a client would become her muse (as had Lily Elsie). In Paris she singled out the actress Monna Delza (who adored fashion) as 'so lovely that it was a joy to dress her, and I always found her an inspiration.'[21]

Designs dating from 1910 to 1913 illustrate Lucile's preoccupation with and mastery of straight sheath styles (known variously as 'Directoire' 'Empire', 'Josephine' or '*Récamier*'). For evening collections she assembled shimmering combinations of lightweight fabrics and trimmings, composed in diaphanous layers, ringing the changes by stylistic adjustments to tunics, sleeves and necklines. In the early 1900s, she began her ploy of setting outer semi-transparent layers over a peach or flesh-pink lining to give the seductive appearance of naked skin. By the 1910s she was the past master of this technique – in 1912 she stipulated: 'The foundation must be of flesh pink, as the whole impression is that the sapphire chiffon is her only covering. It is astonishingly effective.'[22] Related to this provocative practice was her habit of giving overskirts long side slits so that legs could be glimpsed through diaphanous lower layers. With a keen appreciation of textiles, Lucile was omnivorous in her quest for ideas and fabrics. Her newspaper columns in the *New York American Examiner* offer insights into her methodology, recording how she gleaned inspiration from museum collections, advertising signs and, surprisingly for this date, threadbare clothes worn by steerage passengers. She combed unfashionable shops in the ethnic quarters of great cities for trimmings and yardage – idiosyncratically calling her very personal cache of ideas 'my own'.[23] The wearing of distressed, washed-out clothing is now commonplace but Lucile was a pioneer in the use of faded fabrics – as early as 1904 she specified 'faded scarlet cloth' for a walking ensemble. Throughout these years she perfected the skill of creating prototypes by draping lengths of supple textiles straight onto the body (or dressmaker's form). Ingeniously draped gowns resulted – often with intricate fastening arrangements, as each layer was secured in place – while asymmetrically arranged panels and side panniers became Lucile specialities (*left*). Cecil Beaton considered that the Lucile 'creations of this period are surely the loveliest. They are mostly built on Empire lines and are of an unique elaboration. Pastel shades and sweet pea colouring were used with triumphant precision, drapery of filmy chiffon was weighed down with embroidery of almost incredible delicacy, the hems of underskirts revealed sprays of silver-thread wheat and lover's knots of blue.'[24]

Day wear was not neglected and had practical overtones – for summer dresses linens and crisp cottons as well as gauzy lawns and voiles held sway (*above*), while for autumn and winter costumes pliant, smooth-faced wools were preferred. In a notable collection for autumn and winter wear in 1912, costumes were provided with cosy fur edges and huge muffs for protection against the weather, and roomy, sensible pockets (*opposite, left*). Existing understated tailored day wear indicates a preference for grey and

ABOVE Print of a layered Directoire evening gown in embroidered tulle and chiffon. The black-and-white print gave clients a clear idea of the design, with its deep V décolletage, short bodice with knotted sash and swathed asymmetrical overskirt bordered with fleur-de-lys and scattered with roses. Customers could select colours and fabrics as they wished. The fashion drawing resembles the actress Lily Elsie, and the pose, with outstretched arms, imitates another popular postcard of Gabrielle Ray in *The Dollar Princess*.

ABOVE Ink drawing of a summer dress intended for Lucile's younger clientele, 1912. Beneath a broad-brimmed sun hat the dress has an innocent appeal, with its high-waisted, short-sleeved bodice with falling lace collar, and tapered skirt of graduated layers of embroidered muslin appliquéd with a favourite Lucile decorative device: meandering ruched bands. Its price was 26 guineas.

dark navy-blue worsteds made into hip-length jackets and skirts that skimmed over the shoes. Tailored ensembles did not escape Lucile finishing touches, including multiple rows of self-covered buttons, edges piped with contrasting velvet, checked or striped bias bindings and satin linings in vivid colours or bold stripes. Every detail was considered – accessories were crucial. Winter clothes often had dramatically extravagant furs flung around them, whereas in summer the sun's rays were deflected by dainty parasols. Hats bore Lucile labels or were bought in from leading milliners. Lucile favoured elegant court shoes with almond points or Langtry styles with Louis heels and distinctive flared tabs with buckles. She had certain *bêtes noires* – she detested sturdy walking boots of the type worn in the country; in their place she championed shoes of daintier construction and specified they were to be worn with smart yet protective spats.

ABOVE Print of a walking ensemble from the Autumn/Winter 1912–13 collection. This collection featured elaborate fur-edged costumes teamed with gigantic muffs. To heighten its appeal, the fashion artist elongated the complex design of a very short jacket secured by ties slotted through a toggle and tucked behind a belt with its matching, asymmetrically constructed, narrow skirt. The ensemble was later photographed in Lucile's Paris garden on a rather short mannequin, who was overwhelmed by the complicated design, huge muff and unbecoming 'plant pot' hat, with a centre-front aigrette surmounted with a pom-pom (a curious notion for day wear).

ABOVE RIGHT What appears to be a fanciful theatrical costume is in fact a Lucile evening gown. *The Illustrated London News* (June 1913) used the house photograph to explore the theme 'Twixt East and West: Oriental Influence on European Costume'. The weekly paper stated that 'This particular model in which the influence of Persian costume is distinctly noticeable shows us a study of blue tulle veiled with an overskirt of green pailleté chiffon richly embroidered in gold and pearls.' The brocade coat and lofty headdress of plumes and pearls further enhanced the oriental note, as did the combination of fur and filmy fabric.

After surviving the sinking of the *Titanic*, 14 April 1912, and suffering the trauma of press accusations of cowardice, Sir Cosmo and Lady Lucy appeared before the British Board of Trade Inquiry in front of the largest crowd yet seen in the court – 'fashionable women looked down from the side galleries, while the court was bright with Summer toilettes and oppressive with perfumes'. On this grave occasion, Harold Spender of the *Daily News* (whose columns were telegraphed to *The New York Times* on 21 May 1912) included descriptions of high society filling the court and the suitably restrained Lucile attire worn by the witness: 'The white aigrette of Friday last erect and challenging has given place to the sweep of a large black picture hat, shading her eyes to the left and drooping with a hint of tears over the right shoulder. A collar of exquisite lace ripples down from the shapely neck to the waist, very white and vivid against the black dress.' (She wore black for almost all her court appearances.) Husband and wife were exonerated but Lucile detailed the devastating effects the catastrophe had upon them personally; and while she regained control by immersing herself in Lucile Ltd, her husband never wholly recovered. Leaving London, they took solace in the thriving rue de Penthièvre establishment, their Paris apartment, and their residence in Versailles, the Pavillon Mars. In 1913 Lucile Ltd held fashion shows in Paris and New York, surviving programmes revealing a unity of purpose. Languorous mannequins grace the front covers – in New York a photograph captured a sultry beauty in *déshabillé* showing an enticing amount of leg (*see page 191*), while in Paris a fashion illustration depicted an asymmetrical draped, trained, pink evening gown teamed with a towering aigrette headdress. Now aged 50, Lucile's vision remained steady and her capacity for hard work was undiminished, as she continued to create for clients who appreciated her alluring designs and through them, the romance she brought into their lives.

ABOVE LEFT Ink drawing of a presentation gown, *c.*1913, probably by Molyneux for Lucile. An elegant, high-waisted sheath gown in figured silk has a V-necked embroidered bodice with short dolman sleeves, ornate beaded belt and long train. The triple 'Prince of Wales' plumed headdress was *de rigueur*, whereas the *sautoir* of pearls and bouquet of roses were matters of personal choice. As a divorcee Lucile could not attend court but she provided countless exquisite gowns for those who were summoned to appear before royalty. Society's need for presentation dresses, wedding gowns and trousseaux brought Lucile Ltd a regular income.

ABOVE Front cover of a programme for a fashion parade at Lucile's rue de Penthièvre establishment, Paris, 14 October 1913, depicting an evening gown, probably drawn by Molyneux for Lucile. The vogue for high-waisted, svelte gowns was widespread, but those created by Lucile were exceptional, with uniquely draped skirts. Touchingly, in this pre-war collection, she named a tailored grey and black velvet costume 'Cosmo', after her husband, just two years before their separation.

LEFT A tango frock ('My Sweetheart') with chiffon sleeves, fur-edged corselette bodice, overskirt and asymmetrically draped charmeuse skirt with train. In New York, 1913 Lucile showed a collection of these dinner dresses (including this gown) on mannequins wearing her famous brightly coloured wigs. Lucile explained in her fashion column in *Harper's Bazaar* (December 1913) that the trains '…can be hooked up in a manner that makes tangoing possible'.

OPPOSITE Front cover of a programme for a private view of dresses and hats for the Fall Season, New York, 6–8 October 1913. Towards the end of the parade Lucile showed a number of boudoir and tea gowns. It is just possible that this delicately erotic *déshabillé* is 'Afterwards Love' – a chiffon and lace underdress with tea coat worn with a ribbon and lace Lucile boudoir cap. The transparent coatee is ornately embroidered over an insubstantial dress, tantalizingly slit to thigh level revealing legs in silk stockings and pale satin shoes with Louis heels.

Lucile

By Spring 1914 Lucile Ltd was a large, successful, international fashion company with branches in London, Paris and New York. Lucile enjoyed living and working in Paris, and spending weekends in Versailles. In her memoir she describes a joyful and carefree summer, shattered abruptly by the declaration of war on 3 August 1914. A group of finely detailed pencil drawings (*below*) depict the fashionable designs Lucile had prepared for her Autumn 1914 collection, but few orders were placed. Irregular and potentially hazardous shipping, combined with prohibitively high insurance premiums, brought the transportation of private clients, wholesale buyers and fashion exports, to a virtual standstill. Editor-in-Chief of *Vogue*, Edna Woolman Chase wrote: 'Amid the steel and cannon, the bloodshed and the slaughter, the furbelows of the dressmaking business may seem frivolous, but it must be remembered that in France the *couture* is a vital industry… involving thousands of people and millions of francs.'[25] Lucile Ltd was just one of many houses to incur losses.

Lucile recorded for posterity that her intentions to undertake war work were subsumed by an imperative to underwrite the Paris house. America had not yet entered the war and Lucile Ltd was exceptional in having an offshoot in New York, where business was positively thriving. In order to maximize sales, Lucile relocated, taking some of her models with her. She later recalled: 'These War-time years in New York were so crowded that looking back on them is like turning over the leaves of an album of pictures…'[26]

LEFT Pencil drawing of a summer dress banded with lace, accented with a floral corsage and a fringed sash around the high waistline. It is annotated: 'To be made in crêpe de chine' and priced '22 gns'. This demure frock, finished with a *bavolet* (rustic-style cap), is decorated with a bow and tiny millinery flowers. Autumn 1914.

CENTRE Signed and dated pencil drawing of a tailored costume comprising a high-waisted, broad-belted jacket with interesting button tabs that pass through the face of the garment, and a long skirt that tapers towards the hem. Millinery with aigrette and oversize muffs accessorized many of Lucile's outerwear ensembles for Autumn 1914.

RIGHT Signed and dated pencil and watercolour depicting a luxuriant tea gown with an ermine-edged neckline. Pencil annotations reveal that it was trimmed with silver braid; lined in green chiffon (silk would have been used); and cost 10 guineas. A faint pencil sketch reveals the draped back of this *deshabillé*. Autumn 1914.

Unable to work creatively amidst the bustle of the New York branch, Lucile rented a design studio nearby. Whilst she necessarily subdued her aesthetic for wartime European clients, in New York orders poured in for luxurious fashion: within just three months she was '…literally coining money'.[27] Lucile successfully covered her Paris overheads and opened a new branch in Chicago, at 1400 Lake Shore Drive (1915). In order to keep abreast of demand, the dressmaker engaged four assistant designers: Robert Kalloch, Shirley Barker, Gilbert Clarke and Howard Greer. (Lucile Ltd proved fertile training ground for Clarke and Greer, who later became acclaimed Hollywood costume designers.) Lucile's collections were further enriched by creative input from talented students of costume design at the New York School of Fine and Applied Art (later renamed Parsons School of Design) where she taught from 1915 to 1919.[28]

There are many renditions of designs from Lucile's Autumn 1915 collection housed within the Archive (*opposite*). Greer describes evocatively the gathering of New York's elite invitees attending the fashion parade presented at 160 Fifth Avenue: 'Women in sables, aigrettes, and emeralds fought politely with women in chinchilla, paradise, and diamonds for the best seats. The orchestra started playing. The room was heavy with scent. Programmes crackled between gloved hands. There was an expectant hush, all heads turned towards the entrance, and Madame herself came in. Like royalty she was shown to a chair reserved for her immediately in front of the chiffon-curtained stage. The moment she was seated, the orchestra went into a waltz and the parade of mannequins began.'[29]

The demand for invitations to Lucile's exclusive fashion parades became so great that she hired a theatre where she staged fashion spectacles to audiences two to three thousand strong several afternoons a week (the entrance fee was donated to an actors' benevolent fund). Whilst very few women could afford to order a Lucile gown, clearly many derived pleasure by watching and dreaming. Lucile wrote: 'So the parade went on, three hours of it, morning dresses, tea-gowns, nightdresses covered with exotic boudoir wraps, afternoon dresses for garden parties, evening dresses that made the women in the stalls give little cries of admiration.'[30] She claimed her mantle as 'the established leader of the fashions in America… .'[31]

Meanwhile, in Paris, conditions remained bleak. Recognizing both the plight of the French fashion workers and the interdependence of the Paris and New York industries, Edna Woolman Chase organized a charitable 'Fashion Fête', sponsored by *Vogue*, which was staged in New York in November 1914. Lucile's donation, photographed in *Vogue*, 15 December, was more akin to sober fancy dress than fashion: 'A soldierly suit of wool

khaki trimmed with genuine military buttons and leather belt is "Tommy Aitkins"… .'. Thus followed a series of charity 'fashion fêtes'[32] and fund-raising endeavours, including two fashion revues presented by Lucile, the *Chansons Vivantes* (1916) (*see page 196*) and *Fleurette's Dream at Péronne* (1917). The latter, presented as a matinee at the Little Theatre, related the tale of a destitute French mannequin in the war-torn town that Elinor Glyn had adopted as one of her many wartime charities.

When actress Billie Burke, accompanied by her husband Florenz Ziegfeld, producer of the *Ziegfeld Follies* and *Midnight Frolics*, attended one of Lucile's fashion performances (*c.*1916), he was dazzled by Lucile's designs and Dolores' dramatic presence. Following the show, he arranged to incorporate one of the scenes into his revue, employed Dolores and commissioned Lucile to design costumes. Photographs of her imaginative, sculptural confections for the *Flower* (1917) and *D.E.A.R.E.S.T. Jewel* (1919) pageants are housed in the Archive.[33] The *Jewel* pageant was inspired by the prevailing fashion for bracelets composed of diamonds, emeralds, amethysts, rubies, sapphires and topaz in a pattern which, using the first letter of each jewel, formed the word D.E.A.R.E.S.T. Lucile created costumes to represent each stone. Lucile worked with Ziegfeld until 1922, which generated revenue and broadened her public profile. In addition to producing fanciful costumes, Lucile Ltd continued to receive plentiful orders from actors and performers for fashionable attire to wear on and off stage and screen. Top stars Irene Castle, Isadora Duncan, the Dolly Sisters (identically dressed twins), Mary Pickford, Norma Talmadge, Clara Kimball Young and Pearl White were all clients.

In her public persona Lucile cut an extraordinary figure. Greer, who worked at the design studio, recalled: 'She would arrive around ten o'clock in the morning… accompanied by a chauffeur, a maid, a secretary and the eternal bevy of Pekinese and chows. She affected long, flowing chiffon veils, white suede Russian boots, and Tosca walking sticks.'[34] Conversely, whilst working, 'Madame wore, as was her unalterable custom, a simple, unadorned black knitted dress. Clothes-conscious she might have been for the rest of the world, but for herself, she had little vanity.'[35] Like Worth and Poiret, Lucile postured as an artist, mixed socially within a bohemian milieu and professed naivety about all matters commercial. But, unlike a fine artist, she was compelled to comply with the fashion calendars relentless demands and was contractually bound to design two collections each year before she received any monies from the company.

By 1916, the Hanover Square house in London was struggling to survive, and the launch of British *Vogue* (introduced when American imports ground to a halt), which featured Lucile's designs extensively from the outset, could not have been better timed. The first issue, published

15 September 1916, included a double-page feature headlined: 'Lucile prepares to clothe the world and the stage', prefacing the breadth and sphere of her influence. The second issue – published one month later – highlighted Lucile's eclectic use of historical references: 'Old world and stately, youthful and 1916 – no age is ignored by this versatile designer in pursuit of her mission, the beautifying of women.' In November 1915 an editorial expressed the ephemeral quality of a Lucile gown by pronouncing it so fragile that a puff of wind might easily waft both dress and wearer into thin air. In this, the third issue, Lucile Ltd actively marketed its London house (unusual for such an exclusive house) by placing an advertisement – an eighteenth-century inspired Art Deco graphic designed by 'G.E.M.', for 'Robes. Manteaux. Lingerie.'

Throughout the war years and beyond, the fashion press highlighted Lucile's independent fashion vision and made references to the other-worldly and transformative qualities of her 'original' and 'picturesque' designs. Describing a dress from her Spring 1917 collection, British *Vogue's* editorial eulogized: 'Not only art but consummate skill went into the

LEFT A Lucile feather-bedecked, broad-brimmed straw hat is modelled with allure at a tilted angle. Beneath her tailored costume the mannequin wears a soft lace blouse in a style that was contemporaneously known as a 'pneumonia blouse' because it was open at the front and bared the neck (having succeeded the high-necked blouses formerly in vogue) *c.*1916.

arrangement of this delicious blending of filmy fabrics. It surely must be literally blown together or cunningly cajoled into having an appearance, as its little puffs seem full of air, and the silvery flower flounces just float in space around its fortunate wearer. To think that this has been cut and stitched together is an anomaly which passes the imagination of the uninitiated.'[36] Unfortunately the grim realities of business at Lucile Ltd were far from magical.

In her private life, Lucile had enjoyed a series of liaisons with adoring young men, but when her relationship with a Russian she called 'Bobbie' became more serious, Cosmo could no longer tolerate the situation and in 1915 he left her. Without his moderating influence, her loyalty to the company and its founders started to waver. Subsequently, acting independently, she entered into a business agreement with an Otis F. Wood for the sole right to place her endorsement on articles of clothing (subject to her approval), for which she would receive 50 per cent of the profits. She breached this exclusivity by marketing her name and retaining the profits herself. In December 1917 she was successfully sued at the New

York Court of Appeal: the legal implications of this case in terms of contract law have generated much interest in recent years.[37]

Lucile was impulsive and could be cavalier in business, but she did demonstrate a finely tuned sensitivity to developments in future fashion markets. She actively promoted herself and her designs, diversified her output, entered new markets, licensed her name and endorsed a spectrum of products. Various ventures included writing fashion correspondence columns (which included pieces in *Harper's Bazaar, Good Housekeeping, The Daily Sketch, The Illustrated London News* and four special articles for *Weldon's Ladies' Journal*); designing dashing aviatrix suits for women pilots (1917); appearing on film (in the weekly 'Around the Town' series, produced by Gaumont from 1918);[38] launching a fragrance, 'La Rose Lucile' (1919);[39] as well as offering a personalized perfume service from the Rose Room in New York.

Lucile also disseminated her style to women living across the length and breadth of America who could, via a special 'portfolio' from the Sears, Roebuck mail order company, order a ready-made dress she had designed for about one-tenth the price (around $30) of a Lucile original. The great many women who were accomplished at crochet could incorporate a Lucile-designed yoke or edging to an existing garment or make a complete blouse by purchasing a pattern from the 'Lady-Duff [*sic*] Gordon Series' published by the Richardson Silk Company (Chicago and New York), which cost just 10 cents. In 1917, four pattern books became available: *Crochet Yokes and Blouses, Crochet Edgings and Insertions, Irish and Cluny Crochet* and *Boudoir and Breakfast Caps*. Rather than let copyists profit, the dressmaker recognized that she could undertake these projects without compromising the aura of her precious output. Many of these spin-offs were undertaken using 'Lady Duff Gordon' as the prime credit, legally permitting her to exploit a loophole in her contract and enabling her to bypass the company financially. Whilst she could adapt, and was adept at designing for the mass market on short-term projects, Lucile's preferred metier was luxurious and exclusive.

Lucile's penchant for personalized, romantic dress found eloquent expression in her bridal designs, which were recorded, and generated valuable publicity, in the society pages of ladies' papers. Society weddings, such as that of Daglish-MacDonell, documented by *The Queen* on 28 June 1919, represented significant orders comprising wedding, travelling and bridesmaids' dresses.[40] Possibly the most extravagant wedding order Lucile received was for the daughter of an American millionaire in *c.*1919, which

LEFT A scene from Lucile's fund-raising *Chansons Vivantes*, staged at the Plaza Hotel in New York, 1916, and probably taken during the act 'A Promenade of Modern Fashions'. With one hand placed on a (signature Lucile) ribbon-entwined cane, Dolores (centre) shows a picture hat and a trailing, layered, silk chiffon garment with a handkerchief hemline worn over a 'satin' dress. Photograph: Burke Atwell, Autumn 1915.

RIGHT Pencil sketch of a cape featuring similar cross-over straps to the tailored costume modelled by Phyllis, standing on the right in the left illustration. Lucile's wartime tailoring often referenced uniform: this detail might have been inspired by the crossed red straps on a nurse's cape or a military weight-bearing bandoleer (a broad belt worn over the shoulder and across the breast). The mannequin photographed on the left also wears a single strap not unlike a bandoleer's.

amounted to $30,000, on top of which Lucile additionally demanded – and received – a further $5000 to provide a personal consultation at the weekend.[41] Lucile documented the clothes modelled by Phyllis (and later selected the image of her wearing the bridal gown for her autobiography), and by a child who posed as one of the bridesmaids. A surviving album containing these photographs reveals that the bride was a Miss Tompson; it also provides fascinating insights into the range of ceremonial, formal, intimate, day and evening wear that comprised this memorable order (*see overleaf, top*).[42]

During the early post-war years, the aesthetic, materiality and language of international fashion shifted and trends evolved towards the flapper (or *garçonne*) style, which reached its peak in 1926. 'Practical' and 'sporty' became the desirable adjectives for day wear, and whilst 'exquisite gowning' remained appropriate for evening, the cut and styling of dresses was skilfully simplified (and rendered entirely luxurious, with hand-worked beading and embroidery). The shift dress and two-piece jersey costume became fashion staples: these garments hung loosely from the shoulders, bypassed the waist and hovered over the hips. Hemlines were raised to just below the knee for all occasions. To Lucile it was inconceivable this mode might reflect and reinforce post-war women's greater emancipation: to her it was simply a resourceful response by couturiers to fabric shortages and rising costs: 'No woman… could cost less to clothe!'[43]

In 1919 a dress required just three yards of material to make but, as Lucile bemoaned to a reporter from Britain's *Sunday Express* newspaper, even this quantity of brocaded silk represented £21 of a dress that would sell for between £80 to £100. Labour costs had also rocketed: 'A work girl who earned 4s daily before the war, now expects 12s. Pre-war an apprentice earned £1 a month and her luncheon every day. Now it is £10 a month plus lunch.'[44] Lucile describes how she struggled to make even half of her pre-war profits. However, in May 1919, her personal and company finances were in good shape. Her salary, fees and company dividends provided her with £10,000 a year; the assets of Lucile Ltd showed a surplus of £41,433, and her shares, valued at par, were worth £74,435.[45] It was at this point that Lucile engaged the services of Otto Bernard Shulhof, a wholesale manufacturer, as her agent and attorney, 'to vote the stock' owned by her and, in a separate contract (dated 3 July 1919), the four companies that comprised Lucile Ltd appointed him a director.[46] Lucile agreed to work as a salaried designer before reconciling crucial differences: Shulhof's priorities were mass-market and commercially driven, whilst her

LEFT Pencil drawing of three trimmed, sailor-style straw hats, priced at 3 and 4 guineas, *c.*1915. Pencil annotations for the design on the bottom left specify that the hand-made flowers are to be dyed in the same colour tone as the hat. Decorative, hand-crafted silk flowers were a Lucile Ltd house signature. Describing a flesh-toned silk frock with a girdle in two shades of orchid-coloured silk faille, the 1 December 1919 issue of American *Vogue* wrote: 'The spray of flowers that blooms so daintily at the waist is of silk in pale shades, made with the charm that only comes when Lucile is the gardener.'

RIGHT Watercolour and pencil design, *c.*1917, signed 'Lucile' for 'Miss Shirley Kellogg'. Miss Kellogg was a beautiful actress and singer who made her first appearance on the New York stage in 1908. She moved to London to perform as Cornelia Van Huyt in *The Blue House* at the Hippodrome in 1912, whence her career flourished. Lucile designed this striking red tailored ensemble for her, with its roomy, military-inspired pockets and black fur trim. It is accessorized with a black toque, white belt and black, laced boots. It could have been intended for the stage or worn as 'showy' daywear.

ABOVE LEFT Phyllis is pictured in the fur-trimmed, pearl-embroidered wedding gown Lucile designed for Miss Tompson, 1918–19. Lucile states that the gown cost £600 and the veil of antique lace a further £150. (Lucile refers to both pounds and dollars in her autobiography and this text follows her citation.) Lucile selected this photograph for her autobiography.

ABOVE RIGHT The new bride's trousseau included this peignoir, which was made in sheer blue and silver silk. Howard Greer described the second floor of Lucile's New York house (where Miss Tompson would have selected her lingerie, nightwear and *déshabillé*) in *Designing Male* (1952, p. 43): 'It was called the Rose Room and rightly, for its walls were hung with pink taffeta, over-draped with the frailest lace, and the pink taffeta curtains at the windows and around the day bed were caught up with garlands of satin, taffeta and jewelled flowers.'

BELOW Dolores is modelling – to great effect – a high-collared, satin-weave evening cape embellished with fur bands composed in blocks. Other photographs in this series note the fur was kolinsky (the name given to the long, silky fur of the Asiatic mink, also known as red sable) and the sash was made in clashing blue and orange silk 'satin'. Beneath the reverse collar are suspended two fringed satin 'pendants', each accented with a 'Chinese ornament', Autumn 1917.

passion for individuality and luxury had not abated. New designers were engaged to create less expensive models and the character of the business started to change. Her position became untenable. The dressmaker had forsaken the right to design as 'Lucile' (except in London), was grieving following the death of Bobbie, and no longer had reason to remain in America.

Lucile longed to return to Europe and booked a passage on a ship bound for England. When she arrived at Hanover Square, she learned that fabrics were scarce and orders scant: she took possession of her former studio and worked on creating gowns as cheaply as possible. She was restless (she said her designs were 'desultory'), prompting her to move on to Paris, where the business had been supported by war profiteers and South American clients.

During the war, whenever he was home on leave, Molyneux had designed for Lucile Ltd. Greer credits him with keeping the company '…on a par with the younger and more progressive houses in Paris',[47] and his modern designs were attracting a new clientele. Rather than embrace and build upon this success, which might have provided the company with a future, Lucile issued an ultimatum: either he adhere to her established house style or leave. Molyneux left, and just months later, in November 1919, announced the opening of his new Paris house, complete with beautiful mannequins (including the famous former Lucile employee, Hebe). Molyneux went on to become an international fashion force noted for, amongst other things, stylish evening pyjamas and 'pyjamas tea gowns', successors of the very garment that Lucile had made her own, and dressing actresses (Gertrude Lawrence was a favoured client). Lucile omitted from her memoir the altercation with Molyneux, and he bore her no malice; he had invested in Lucile Ltd by purchasing shares (initially in 1916, and then again in 1921 and 1926),[48] and remained in contact with her for the rest of her life.

There are few examples of Lucile's designs on paper or photographs in the Archive from the early 1920s. However, between 1920 and 1922, her collections received extensive coverage in the fashion media and in November 1920 she staged a fashion parade at London's exclusive Hyde Park Hotel. Sporting and menswear influences, laced with a romantic flourish, were manifest in her tan-coloured leather jacket, plaid kilt and dark-green velvet shooting coat shown in *Vogue* in January 1920, where they were interpreted as '…an impudent and dainty mockery of masculine apparel, with their severe blouses of heavy white silk, with large vague collars such as Byron himself might have found almost too picturesque to suit even his romantic taste.'[49] By contrast, evaluating Chanel's collection, which was imbued with similar influences, *Vogue* noted (the same year): 'This house shows no striking novelties, sponsors, no daring or extreme modes, but presents eminently wearable and well-designed costumes…

ABOVE LEFT A high-necked, fur-trimmed evening cloak, made in pink silk brocaded with rose motifs and decorative tassels, was ordered for 'going-away'. These photographs were taken at the 'Lucile Ltd Studio' at her 160 Fifth Avenue house, New York.

ABOVE RIGHT Miss Tompson ordered this smart, protective, motoring coat with striped fabric detailing to wear on her honeymoon. To protect her head, she probably wore a long veil pinned to her millinery, pulled down over the ears and tied around her neck. (Goggles were available but were generally unpopular with fashionable women). A plethora of luxurious leather, fur and wool accessories was also offered to ensure warmth and protection from dirt, wind and rain.

BELOW Dolores' striking profile pose creates drama and shows Lucile's abundant fur coat, with deep collar made in a contrasting pelt, to great advantage. Such a garment was glamorous, epitomized luxury and was a great status symbol. It is likely that Lucile designed it and sent it to a skilled furrier to be made. It is worn over a spangled, fine silk dress that swathes around the ankles. Photograph: New York, Autumn 1917.

Model N° 44

Chinchilla
yellow cloth

tarnished trimming
yellow chiffon

black
blue violet

Chinese ornament
in all shades
of blue lavender
black satin

PREVIOUS PAGE Dinarzade wears an ornate, blue and yellow cloth, silk satin and chiffon ensemble, accented with a 'Chinese ornament'. It has sheer silk sleeves and a chinchilla fur trim, and is accessorized with a fur-crowned beret and fur neckpiece. Lucile had a penchant for oriental styling combined with unusual fabric juxtapositions, and she regularly revived such styling throughout the remainder of her career. Photograph: New York, Autumn 1917.

TOP Embossed photograph of Arjamand gazing dreamily into the foreground, her face framed by a ribbon-trimmed cartwheel hat. Lucile's tailored day wear was stylish, restrained and unerringly elegant. Her use of a contrasting coloured fabric directs attention to the high waistline and pocket flaps: on the sleeves it has been utilized to resemble gauntlet gloves. The narrow skirt reaches just above the ankle, facilitating ease of movement. Photograph: New York, Spring 1918.

BOTTOM The alluring Arjamand models a daytime dress with subtle, irregular striping and medallion-like motifs on the bodice. Although it has tassel-tipped, draped hood, she wears a pert, feather-trimmed hat. On her feet are ribbon-laced, Louis-heeled, silk-satin shoes that match the dress. Photograph: New York, Spring 1918.

Howard Greer described Arjamand as 'the first of the really emaciated mannequins ever to model fashionable clothes. She was so thin that we used to make cracks about stuffing cotton wool between her vertebrae so that people wouldn't think she was a skeleton.' (*Designing Male*, p.40)

OPPOSITE A restrained, lightweight duster coat is styled to engulf the mannequin (both the garment and the way it is styled for photography look entirely modern). Duster coats provided protection from the clouds of dust that could be raised when travelling by automobile in the dry summer months. Camouflage 'dust shades' of beige, fawn, cream or grey were most popular. The finest quality coats were made of tussore silk, which is lightweight, durable and drapes well. Lucile's rendition combines style with utility. Protection for the head is provided by a fashionable, plumed beretta. Photograph: New York, Spring 1918.

each model at this house suits an amazing variety of types.'[50] (It is perhaps pertinent to note that whilst Chanel captured fashion's zeitgeist, the costumes she designed for Hollywood films in 1931 and 1932 were generally disliked by the stars and disappointed Depression audiences – because of their understatement). Lucile, meanwhile, retained her ethos of individual expression in fashion which, as always, was most apparent in evening wear.

A feature titled 'Lucile finds inspiration in epochs of romance', published in American *Vogue*, January 1921, might equally have been written in 1905: 'Lucile's winter opening for her clients reminds one of a theatrical representation and is suitably shown on her small stage, hung with curtains of dull blue backed with vivid green. One entirely forgets the mode as such, and thinks of each model as a *tableau vivant* complete in itself, each one designed to enhance the charm of a lovely woman… Everything that can add feminine beauty is found in these gowns – laces, furs, softly brilliant embroideries in coloured silks, and gold, silver, and copper. The evening gowns have an air of spurning considerations of practicality and rejoicing in their gorgeousness.'[51] This last sentence might have been a metaphor for the fate of Lucile Ltd.

Surprisingly, perhaps, it was the American branches of Lucile Ltd that were the first to fold. Early in 1921 the Chicago branch was closed. In 1922 the New York company was declared bankrupt (and finally dissolved in February 1932).[52] The press reported that Lucile Ltd, including the staff of over a hundred, had been taken over by fashion 'importing and speciality house' J.M. Giddings & Co, of 724 Fifth Avenue, New York. Lucile no longer had any active connection with the firm, but Evelyn McHorter, premier designer for Lucile, and Guy H. Tolman, former director, were retained to supervise the dressmaking and tailoring salons where they would show their creations, alongside a selection of Parisian couture clothing.[53] In August 1922 Lucile was dismissed by the French company and the following year was taken to court for unpaid debts. Questioned under oath about why she was dismissed, she declared: 'Because I told the truth and said that the dresses which they were showing were not designed by me.' (Her admission had been published in a New York newspaper.) Shulhof claimed that she was also indebted to the company for the sum of £21,115, which she, in turn, counterclaimed. On 27 October 1922 Lucile, described in *The Times* as 'dressmaker of Hanover Square', was adjudged bankrupt with gross liabilities of £41,515 and just £396 of assets. When the Assistant Official Receiver had enquired about her share-holdings in Lucile Ltd, she disingenuously announced: 'It is all Greek to me. I don't know what a share is.'[54] On 18 April 1923 she made an application for an order of discharge at the Bankruptcy Court, which was granted, subject to her paying £250.[55]

In December 1922 the British Broadcasting Company was launched, and on 2 May 1923, the first *Women's Hour* (a forerunner of *Woman's Hour*) was broadcast: the invited guest was Lucile, talking about fashion. She was now 60 and London became her final permanent residence. She was visited by an aspiring theatre designer, the young Norman Hartnell, who encountered her '…temporarily installed in a small flat in Park Place, St James's, and on entering a stuffy, dimly-lit room I found this celebrated lady to be rather advanced in years. A green and silver tissue turban surmounted a wealth of bright red hair which drooped on either side of her face… '.[56] Lucile examined (and retained) his designs, and rather imperiously promised him a career in fashion. Whilst waiting to hear from her, Hartnell noticed one of his designs published in a 'My Dear Dorothy' column she wrote for *The Sketch*, which she claimed to be her own creation. Hartnell contacted her but heard nothing. When this scenario was repeated twice more, he took her to court and settled for a modest payment of £50 in his favour.[57]

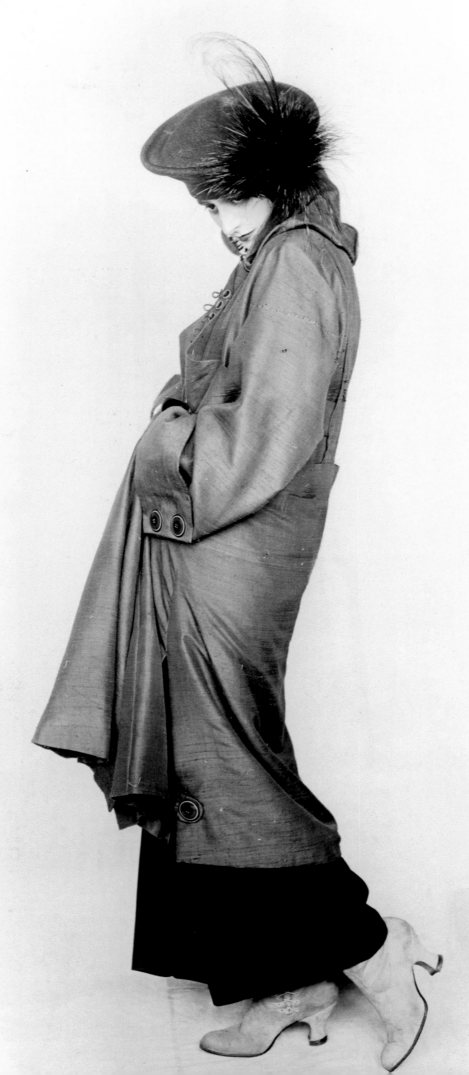

LUCILE L

Alone, and relatively impoverished, Lucile found solace designing dreamy gowns inspired by her imaginings of the dress worn in distant lands and long ago. In the late March 1923 issue of British Vogue, two 'Decorative Frocks from Lucile' were featured: one was described as 'A fantasy from China, which might well have stepped from some old legend from the sacred city', while the other evoked, 'a picturesque gown of cloth of silver', 'The memory of Winterhalter's portrait of the Empress Eugenie surrounded by the lovely women of the court...' Lucile was no longer in fashion's vanguard: if correctly nurtured, Hartnell, like Molyneux before him, might have forged the company's legacy. But instead, Harnell, too, found his own path: he opened a fashion house in 1923 and became one of London's most famous designers.

In 1924 the London house of Lucile Ltd closed. Lucile earned a much-reduced living by designing for a few private clients from a studio apartment at 6, Rossetti Gardens Mansions, Chelsea, writing and teaching. In 1927 she taught in New York at the Cooper Union and Trapenhagen schools of fashion, and the Archive houses some 200 student designs, some with her own hand-written responses. Stamped onto the reverse of some designs is Lucile's New York house logo, which is odd, as the house had closed by then – but perhaps she had another venture in mind (opposite).

Lucile retained her drive, ambition and joy working as an exclusive dressmaker. With generous financial support of her family, including her sister Elinor, in 1928 she registered a new company: the 'court dressmaker' Lucy Duff Gordon Limited was incorporated on 12 April with a nominal capital of £4,000.[58] The Post Office Trades Directories for 1929, 1930 and 1931 list her address as 120 New Bond Street, London W1 – London's most exclusive fashion thoroughfare. The Archive houses a number of water-colours with fabric snips attached from this period (opposite).

In 1930, using the name Lady Duff Gordon, Lucile wrote three articles for Weldon's Ladies' Journal (July, August and September), whose editorial prefaced her as 'The world-renowned fashion writer and designer.' Alongside advice on which fabrics to select to make up the company's paper patterns, she shared confidences with her readers: 'Girls, don't you just adore making your own frocks and "undies", as they are generally called, or "withins", as I call them?'; and, stressing her awareness of her readers' need for economy, suggested they update a morocain dress by removing the sleeves to make a cape. She was emphatic (July and August) that a woman must always look her best when travelling by choosing matching outfits and luggage in brown or beige tones – the colour of 'travel stains'.

BELOW Pencil and watercolour depiction of an evening dress, with snips of green and black gauzy silk and a scattered floral printed silk georgette, attached, 1928–9. This is one of a series of designs prepared for 'Lucy Duff Gordon Ltd'. Gracefully rendered, it depicts a *robe de style* with pagoda sleeves and bears the dressmaker's hallmark layering, sheer fabrics and bow detailing. Red shoes echo the fashion figure's red-painted hair.

BELOW RIGHT Pencil sketches, on Lucile's headed paper, for a draped 'cyclamen' dress and open-crowned turban with oriental overtones, *c.*1928. These finely drawn designs, depicted on an elongated fashion body, perfectly convey the filmy fabric; asymmetric cut with thin straps encircling the upper arm; and fringing and tassels.

In 1931, the second autobiography written by Frances, Countess of Warwick, was published. She was an intriguing aristocrat who was converted to socialism and who invited Elinor to a number of her house parties. It was called *Discretions*. In a chapter entitled 'Mainly Feminine', she wrote that whilst the middle classes were infinitely better dressed, if one were to compare present-day fashions with those of her Edwardian youth, 'The upper classes are less well dressed, in the sense that that clothes are less individual, and their "creations" and "exclusive designs" have almost gone out of fashion… .'[59] In October 1931 the fashion enterprise Lucy Duff Gordon Ltd was wound up voluntarily, the process completed by 31 August 1932, and in 1932 affairs at the Paris house also terminated.[60] Sir Cosmo Duff Gordon died in 1931. By 1932 the name of Lucile was no longer listed in London Post Office Trade Directories – only Lady Duff Gordon's apartment at Rossetti Gardens Mansions, in the Street Directories. By 1933 there are no references. She had been diagnosed with breast cancer, and resided in a London nursing home until her death on 17 April 1935. She was buried alongside Cosmo at Brookwood Cemetery, London.

BELOW LEFT Watercolour design for a black evening dress, *c.*1929. Lucile's version of the little black dress has godets inserted into the sheer sleeves, as well as an uneven hemline to create petal-like shapes that would have fluttered when animated. The flame-red wig takes to extremes Lucile's natural red hair. In her autobiography, Lucile claimed to have launched the vogue for coloured wigs in around 1911: 'Every smart woman wanted one of these *têtes de couleurs*, as they were called, to wear in the evening. It was a queer, exotic caprice of mine, but it caught on. The wigs matched the dresses, a rose pink with a dress of deeper pink, a jade green with a dress of emerald. The coloured heads bobbing about a dance floor made it look like a flower garden….' She continued to show coloured wigs with her designs for the rest of her career.

BELOW Pencil and watercolour design for a full-length, lace-trimmed, bias-cut evening dress with a white sash priced at 32 guineas, *c.*1930. A swatch of flesh-toned silk tulle is attached. In *Weldon's Ladies' Journal* (June 1930) Lucile advised readers: 'For colouring, you can always be sure of success if you choose a nude shade of pink trimmed with biscuit lace and pink ribbons.' Throughout her career Lucile advocated the allure of clothing the body whilst suggesting nudity. This is one of the last examples of Lucile's designs in the Archive. It is executed in the same media as her 1905 album.

Appendices

The V&A's Lucile Archive

The Lucile Archive housed in the V&A's Archive of Art and Design comprises over 1,300 paper documents dating from 1904 to 1933, arranged in folders. Presented to the Museum by Lucile's grandson, the late Earl of Halsbury, FRS, it is the largest archive of her work held in Europe and is unique in its scope. This appendix lists the contents in chronological order, highlights the diversity of the material and, through extended captions, analyses Lucile's interiors and other aspects of her business in greater depth. Garments by Lucile, together with the Autumn 1904 and Autumn 1905 fashion albums, are kept in the Furniture, Textiles and Dress Collection.

The Archive encompasses original pencil fashion drawings and watercolour designs, and photographs of the finished fashion and costume ensembles worn by mannequins and actresses. There are some items of business literature such as mannequin parade programmes and press clippings. Further folders include photographs of fancy-dress ensembles; original drawings for the theatre; photographs of flamboyant costumes for the *Ziegfeld Follies*; albums of watercolour fashion drawings with fabric samples; and prints from drawings that were reproduced for clients.

There are also fascinating and intriguing sketches and designs by Edward Molyneux. Whilst there are no explicit references to Normal Hartnell or Howard Greer, it is possible that some of the designs are by them.

The Archive is rich and diverse, and the potential for future research is considerable. Figure numbers refer to the illustrations on pages 208-11.

ACKNOWLEDGEMENTS
With deepest gratitude to Sonnet Stanfill for starting me on this amazing journey with Lucile, Lady Duff Gordon, the archive and her superior generosity of time and encouragement. I am indebted to Jeremy Aynsley and Christopher Breward for their wisdom, guidance, and support whilst writing my MA dissertation on Lucile Ltd. I am grateful to many people for their assistance and generosity especially Caroline Evans and Madeleine Ginsburg and the many curators and collections that have been the utmost of help for my research: Anne Bissonnette, Kent State University Museum; Dilys Blum, Philadelphia Museum of Art; Tim Long and Megan Smith, Chicago History Museum and Molly Sorkin, Fashion Institute of Technology. My thanks extend to V&A colleagues Charlotte Anderson, Glenn Adamson, Oriole Cullen, and Suzanne Smith. Other colleagues to be acknowledged are Susan Aberth, Michelle Major, Patricia Mears, Gity Monsef and Dave Shein. I am eternally grateful to Robin Safer, Rita Shapero, and my father for their undying support. To Amy de la Haye and Valerie Mendes who have been a joy and an inspiration to work with on this book.
SAMANTHA ERIN SAFER

LUCILE LTD ARCHIVE – AAD/2008/6
SKETCHBOOKS 1904–C.1915
TWO FILES

AAD/2008/6/1 SKETCHBOOKS, 1904
Two Lucile sketchbooks, one from her stay at the Villa Trianon in Versailles during the summer of 1904, which includes ephemera, pencil and watercolour drawings. The other sketchbook includes pencil drawings of models (ensembles) from 1904 with fabrics, trimmings and accessories. (figs. 3 and 17)

AAD/2008/6/2 SKETCHBOOKS, 1909–15
Three sketchbooks, one of which is attributed to Edward Molyneux, include pencil drawings, painted daubs of delicate watercolours, and drawings of coats and dresses. Some designs identify the clients as actresses Lily Elsie and Gertie Millar.

DRAWINGS: DESIGNS FOR FASHION AND THEATRE C.1907–1933
EIGHTEEN FILES

AAD/2008/6/3 PENCIL FASHION DRAWINGS, 1907–10
Seventy-two pencil fashion drawings that have model numbers 2–89 written on them; some have additional information pertaining to the design, such as colour, fabric and trim.

AAD/2008/6/4 LILY ELSIE THEATRE DESIGNS, MARCH 1910
Seven pencil sketches of Lily Elsie designs that could have been for Hood and Ross's operetta, *The Count of Luxembourg*, which opened in 1911 at Daly's Theatre. The drawings feature hand-written annotations specifying the colour and fabric used in the gowns. (fig. 22)

AAD/2008/6/5 LUCILE ORIGINAL INK DRAWINGS, 1910–12
Twenty-three original ink drawings of accessorized ensembles. Hand-written annotations identify fabric, colour and trimmings, as well as the number of copies to be made and of what size, indicating that they were reproduced for clients and press.

AAD/2008/6/6 PENCIL FASHION DRAWINGS, 1910–13
Twenty-one pencil drawings of day and evening fashions with accessories. Some drawings have fabric samples attached, and hand-written annotations specifying colour, fabric, client name and/or model number.

AAD/2008/6/7 LUCILE LINGERIE AND NIGHTWEAR DESIGNS, 1910–13, 1915, 1920
Forty-three pencil, colour and ink drawings of petticoats, tea gowns, nightcaps, nightwear and a coverlet/ bedcover/eiderdown design, all signed 'Lucile'. Some drawings have fabric samples attached, and hand-written annotations describing colour, fabric, cut, model number, measurements and client name. (figs. 6 and 15d)

AAD/2008/6/8 MOLYNEUX WATERCOLOUR DESIGNS FOR THEATRE, WITH SOME FASHION, 1911–16
Forty-four watercolour drawings that feature full ensembles with accessories. Some drawings have hand-written annotations on them as well as the client's name. Three magazine cuttings of Molyneux fashion plates. (fig. 26)

AAD/2008/6/9 FASHION PENCIL DRAWINGS, 1912
Twenty-five fashion pencil drawings, with some hand-written annotations on the back stating fabric, colour, price and model number.

AAD/2008/6/10 SKETCHES FOR FASHION AND THEATRE, 1912–13
Nineteen sketches for fashion and theatre designs executed in watercolour and pencil. Some sketches have hand-written annotations on them with customer information, model or number, or references to a play.

AAD/2008/6/11 THEATRE WATERCOLOURS AND FASHION SKETCHES, 1912–15
Twenty-three theatre watercolour designs and fashion sketches, including some Molyneux designs. A few of the drawings have hand-written annotations stating the client's name (among them Gertie Millar and Miss Levy). (fig. 19)

AAD/2008/6/12 FASHION AND THEATRE PENCIL DRAWINGS, 1913–15
Eighty-one pencil drawings, which feature designs for dresses, skirts and hats, signed 'Lucile'. Some drawings have fabric samples attached, and hand-written annotations specifying colour, fabric and accessories, and the number of copies of the drawings that were to be produced. Theatre drawings identify the act in which ensembles were worn, and by whom. (figs. 23 and 28)

AAD/2008/6/13 THEATRICAL DRAWINGS, 1920s
Ten oversized theatrical drawings stamped 'Lucy Duff Gordon'. They include hand-written annotations in pencil.

AAD/2008/6/14 PEN AND COLOUR WASH DRAWINGS, 1920s
Eleven drawings, some with clients' names on them, fabric samples attached, and hand-written annotations in pencil on the reverse.

AAD/2008/6/15 MODELS 1–109 SERIES, 1926–5,
One hundred and twenty-five watercolour drawings with fabric samples.

AAD/2008/6/16 DAVE COX, 1927
Thirteen oversized coloured drawings, including the work of two other artists.

AAD/2008/6/17 STUDENT COLOURED DRAWINGS, 1927–8
Lucile taught fashion design classes at Cooper Union and the Trapenhagen School of Fashion, both located in

New York City. There are 180 drawings in the collection, with students' names and descriptions of the drawings, as well as Lucile's hand-written comments on a number of the designs.

AAD/2008/6/18 LUCILE DESIGNS WITH COLOUR FABRIC SNIPPETS, ALBUM 1928
Forty-six coloured fashion drawings with fabric samples attached, some of which are annotated.

AAD/2008/6/19 LUCILE DESIGNS, 1930–3
Nine coloured drawings of designs, six of which are drawn on '6 Rossetti Gardens Mansions sw3' letter paper, showing the outline of the body.

AAD/2008/6/20 VARIOUS OUTSIZE ITEMS (N.D.)
Three Edward Molyneux drawings in pencil and ink, two miscellaneous fashion drawings and one Henri Manuel photograph of a mannequin modelling a Lucile ensemble.

PRINTS FROM DRAWINGS c.1912–c.1919
SIX FILES

AAD/2008/6/21 FASHION PRINTS FROM DRAWINGS: COPIES OF DESIGNS TO BE SENT TO CLIENTS, 1912
Eighty-one prints from drawings, signed 'Lucile', of model numbers 1–97 to be sent to customers. Some drawings have hand-written annotations on the face or reverse providing date and garment details.

AAD/2008/6/22 FASHION PRINTS FROM DRAWINGS: COPIES OF DESIGNS TO BE SENT TO CLIENTS, 1912
One hundred and fifty-seven prints (including some ink originals) from drawings featuring model numbers 1–124 for the Spring/Summer season, signed 'Lucile'. Some prints have hand-written annotations in pencil or ink describing colour, material, name of ensemble and fabric samples.

AAD/2008/6/23 PRINTS FROM DRAWINGS: COPIES OF DESIGNS TO BE SENT TO CLIENTS, 1912–13
Forty-eight prints from drawings of designs to be sent to clients, including some original ink drawings signed 'Lucile'. Hand-written annotations on the prints variously note the number of copies to be made, model number, date, description and dress name.

AAD/2008/6/24 PRINTS FROM DRAWINGS: COPIES OF DESIGNS TO BE SENT TO CLIENTS, NUMBERS 4–93A, 1912–13
Fifty-three prints from drawings of designs to be sent to customers featuring model numbers 4–93a, all signed or stamped 'Lucile Ltd'. Some hand-written annotations feature on the reverse of the prints, which include model number, fabric and colour description and name of the design.

AAD/2008/6/25 FASHION PRINTS FROM DRAWINGS: COPIES OF DESIGNS TO BE SENT TO CLIENTS, NUMBERS 1–59, 1914
One hundred and twenty-six prints from drawings for clients, all signed 'Lucile' and embossed. Many include names of the designs and model numbers. Some have hand-written pencil annotations with fabric and colour description as well as fabric samples.

AAD/2008/6/26 FASHION PRINTS FROM DRAWINGS: COPIES OF DESIGNS TO BE SENT TO CLIENTS, 1915–19
One hundred and eleven prints from drawings for clients and house use, signed 'Lucile'. Some prints include the model number and name of the ensemble, either on the front of the print or back. (Items in this folder relate to fashion photographs from 1917.)

PHOTOGRAPHS: FASHION, THEATRICAL AND FANCY DRESS 1904–1919
SIXTEEN FILES

AAD/2008/6/27 PHOTOGRAPHS AND COLOURED DRAWINGS, 1904–5
Five coloured fashion drawings and six black-and-white photographs. (figs. 15a and b)

AAD/2008/6/28 MEMENTO ALBUM, 1910–16
Sixty-one black-and-white photographs in the album featuring mannequins posed in the garden of Lucile Ltd, Paris, taken by Henri Manuel. Other photographs are of a mannequin parade in the Paris house, various Paris interior images, customers being fitted, Lucile styling a mannequin, and a New York house interior. Three photographs are mannequins in designs for Lily Elsie. (figs. 2, 4, 5, 7, 9, 10, 11, 13, 15c and 21)

AAD/2008/6/29 HENRI MANUEL PHOTOGRAPHS, 1911–15
Ten photographs of Lucile's mannequins modelling designs and accessories, taken by Henri Manuel inside Lucile Ltd, Paris and outside in the garden.

AAD/2008/6/30 FASHION PHOTOGRAPHS, PARIS, 1912
Twenty-one black-and-white photographs of Lucile models taken in the garden of Lucile, Ltd, Paris. Some of the photographs were featured in Good Housekeeping and others are from the same photographic shoot. (fig. 1)

AAD/2008/6/31 FASHION PHOTOGRAPHS, LONDON AND PARIS, 1912–15
Thirty-nine black-and-white and sepia-tone photographs of mannequins taken inside and outside the Paris house, in the gardens of the London and Paris establishments, and some studio shots (including hats and shoes). (fig. 8)

AAD/2008/6/32 PHOTOGRAPHS OF LUCILE DESIGNS FOR IRENE CASTLE, 1914–17
Fifteen black-and-white photographs of Irene Castle ensembles designed by Lucile.

AAD/2008/6/33 PHOTOGRAPHS OF MODELS AUTUMN 1915, AND GOWNS FOR FLORENCE WALTON
Two hundred and forty-four black-and-white photographs by Burke Atwell, as well as reproductions of the photographs. The photographs depict the collection of 1915 as well as items for dancer Florence Walton, which are labelled accordingly and taken by Ira L. Hills Studio. Information about the ensembles is written in ink and provides the name of the gown, model number and a description. (fig. 27)

AAD/2008/6/34 TABLEAUX VIVANTS I, 1916 (IN AID OF THE WAR ORPHANS OF FRANCE), AND FANCY DRESS
The album contains material about the Orphelinat des Armées and Lucile's involvement with the charity for orphans, as well as the poem 'Lilies of France' by 'H.M.K.S.'. The rest of the album contains 60 black-and-white photographs of mannequins dressed in Lucile designs with an oriental theme as well as fancy-dress ensembles. (fig. 12)

AAD/2008/6/35 TABLEAUX VIVANTS II, 1916, FANCY DRESS AND MISS TOMPSON'S WEDDING c.1919
The album contains 57 black-and-white photographs for fancy-dress designs and a bridal order for Miss Tompson. The fancy-dress images are mainly duplicates from the first Tableaux Vivants album, whilst Lucile mannequin Phyllis models Miss Tompson's wedding trousseau and going-away clothes.

AAD/2008/6/36 FASHION PHOTOGRAPHS I AND II, 1917
One hundred and ninety-one black-and-white photographs of Lucile mannequins, including Phyllis and Dolores, modelling fashions from 1917 in a studio. Some photographs include names of ensembles and model numbers.

AAD/2008/6/37 'LADY DUFF GORDON'S VAUDEVILLE ACT ALBUM', 1917
Large format album with 18 black-and-white photographs mounted on paper featuring Lucile's vaudeville act Fleurette's Dream at Peronne, to benefit the Secours Franco-Americain pour la France Devastée. The act was performed in New York at the Booth Theatre on 18 and 19 October. All photographs are signed 'Lady Duff Gordon, New York'. (fig. 25)

AAD/2008/6/38 LUCILE DESIGNS FOR THE ZIEGFELD FOLLIES, 1917
Seventy-four black-and-white photographs featuring designs for the Ziegfeld Follies scenes entitled 'Flower Chiffon', 'Arabian' and 'Chinese', which are all stamped 'Lucile Ltd' and modelled by Lucile mannequins. Men's 'exotic' fancy dress is also included. (fig. 20)

AAD/2008/6/39 PHOTOGRAPHS OF MODELS, AUTUMN 1917, NEW YORK
The album contains 160 black-and-white photographs of the Autumn 1917 collection for New York, modelled by Lucile's famous mannequins Phyllis, Dolores and Arjamand. Model numbers are written on the top right-hand side of the photographs and include hand-written annotations in black ink.

AAD/2008/6/40 PHOTOGRAPHS OF MODELS, SPRING 1918, NEW YORK
The album includes 221 black-and-white photographs of the 1918 New York collection, with front, back and side views of some ensembles. The model number is written on the top right-hand side of the photographs. Most photographs are annotated. (fig. 14)

AAD/2008/6/41 ZIEGFELD FROLIC, D.E.A.R.E.S.T JEWEL DRESSES, 1919
Fifteen black-and-white photographs of costumes. Each costume has two photographs showing different aspects. Some photographs have hand-written annotations in pencil at the top on the card.

PRESS CUTTINGS, BUSINESS LITERATURE AND INSPIRATIONAL MATERIAL
c.1904–1928
FOUR FILES

AAD/2008/6/42 LUCILE LTD BUSINESS LITERATURE/MANNEQUIN PARADE PROGRAMMES, SPANNING THE PERIOD 1904–18.
Lucile business literature, which includes mannequin parade programmes, theatre orders and sketches from women who applied for the position of a fashion artist in 1912, as well as stationery. (fig. 16, 18, 24)

AAD/2008/6/43 PRESS CLIPPINGS, 1909–28
Various press clippings from newspapers and magazines such as Hearth and Home, Daily Express, Ladies' Pictorial, Vogue and the New York American Examiner.

AAD/2008/6/44 PHOTOGRAPHS TAKEN AT THE RACES AND MISCELLANEOUS INSPIRATIONAL DOCUMENTS/ MISCELLANEOUS PHOTOGRAPHS
Twenty items, which include eight unknown black-and-white photographs, ten black-and-white photographs taken at the races in England, one drawing and one print.

AAD/2008/6/45 PHOTOGRAPHS OF ACTRESSES, 1900–10
Four black-and-white photographs of actresses preserved for inspiration.

Fig. 1 AAD/2008/6/30
This staged photograph, taken in the garden of the Paris house, depicts the 'Modes of Today in Tea Apparel', which featured in Lucile's *Good Housekeeping* column 'Her Wardrobe' in December 1912. Lucile declared that these tea dresses were intended for the winter months and would clothe *le monde chic*. The styling of this photograph is indicative of a contemporary trend for employing the theatrical *tableau vivant* convention to portray a specific house image; Lucile used many such photographs in her contributions to *Good Housekeeping*.

Fig. 4 AAD/2008/6/28
This photograph was taken inside the Paris house, *c.*1911–13. The carpet's pattern echoes the Lucile logo, with ribbons and garlands of flowers. The mannequin, posing as an aristocratic woman, stands in the doorway next to an elegant table. She regards the camera confidently and places one foot forward to show her feathered mules. The wall's moulding provides a decorative backdrop. This image is geared to represent a particular lifestyle, and a certain theatricality. The end result is a seductive sales package.

Fig. 2 AAD/2008/6/28
The Parlour Room in the New York house at 37–9 West 57th Street, *c.*1912–14. Lucile recorded in her autobiography that her great friend Elsie de Wolfe designed the Rose Room and the rest of the interiors in accordance with her requirements and colour schemes. This room bears the hallmarks of de Wolfe's aesthetic, including the use of antique and reproduction furniture, grey panelled walls, contemporary objects, a marble fireplace, wall sconces and large mirrors.

Fig. 5 AAD/2008/6/28
Backstage at a Paris mannequin parade, *c.*1911–14. In her autobiography (p.68), she recalled first envisaging '…a mannequin parade, which would be as entertaining to watch as a play. I would have glorious, goddess-like girls, who would walk to and fro dressed in my models, displaying them to the best advantage to an admiring audience of women.' This photograph shows the organization and seemingly calm atmosphere of the backstage area of the parade. The mannequin Gamela is helped into her blouse by a house *vendeuse* as another mannequin is waiting her turn to walk the stage; a third mannequin sits and chats on the stairs. Lucile's chiffon and lace creations, along with accessories, hang in an orderly manner in the cabinets installed especially for this purpose.

Fig. 3 AAD/2008/6/1
These lists of poetic titles and mannequins' names appear in Lucile's sketchbook dated 1904. They are ideas for titles of her famous named dresses, which Lucile called 'gowns of emotion'. Names such as 'A Sighing Sound of Lips Unsatisfied', 'Delicious Symphonies' and 'Pleasures Thrall' added to the heady mix of frothy chiffon, lace and trimmings of her gowns. Lucile's penchant for naming went beyond her ensembles: to evoke an aura of glamour, exoticism and mystery, she rechristened her house mannequins Hebe, Gamela, Mizella, Dinarzade and Myra.

Fig. 6 AAD/2008/6/7
Pencil drawing of a satin bedspread with trimmings of lace and hand-made flowers *c.*1910–15. Lucile loved interior designs and over the years spent much of her fortune redecorating her homes in London, Paris, Versailles and New York. Every detail was carefully considered. When she came to New York in 1910 to open her house on West Street, on 23 January the editor of the *New York American Examiner* informed its readers: 'The London house of the Duff Gordon's is in Lennox Gardens and is noted in fashionable society for the beauty of its furniture and decoration, which were of course designed by Lady Duff-Gordon.' This drawing is the only soft furnishing design in the Archive, but it reveals that she devoted the same care and attention to furnishing accessories as she did to Lucile gowns. The design is for a customer, but it is similar to the bedspreads that adorned day beds in the 'Rose Rooms' in all her houses, where nightdresses, chemises and other undergarments could be purchased.

Fig. 7 and 8 AAD/2008/6/28; AAD/2008/6/31

Lucile utilized both the interiors and exteriors of her London and Paris houses for her mannequin parades. For the photograph on the left, taken in 1913 in the lush garden of 23 Hanover Square, the models are posed in an organized fashion with parasols as props. Clients sat on the surrounding benches examining this Spring collection. The photograph of Phyllis wearing the same gingham ensemble illustrates a custom of the house to accessorize the mannequins fully for both the parades and the studio photographs. These two images also reveal the reproduction process favoured by Lucile Ltd, from mannequin parade to studio photograph. The photograph, later published in *Harper's Bazaar* (August 1914), served as a house record and client information, as well as illustrative material for Lucile's columns in *Harper's Bazaar* and the *New York American Examiner*.

Fig. 9 AAD/2008/6/28

To fit with her individually conceived 'personality' creations for a client, rooms at Lucile Ltd were designed to suggest different scenes, moods or characters, and here gowns, undergarments and accessories were tried on and bought during conversation and the taking of tea. In these rooms, Lucile was experimenting with the convention of shop-window dressing, carefully choosing items of furniture and draping each room with textiles; this approach mirrored her procedure of selecting appropriate accessories for an ensemble and draping clothes on her mannequins.

Fig. 10 AAD/2008/6/28

Four mannequins are posed outside 11 rue de Penthièvre, Paris, Lucile Ltd's '*grande couture*' house. Fashion and architecture harmonize to achieve a distinctive image, which was Lucile's intention. She took care to choose buildings and interiors that complied with her aesthetic. 'The new Paris house of Lady Duff Gordon is entirely in the period of Louis Philippe, and the new empire fashions are delightfully displayed in such an environment.'[1]

Fig. 15a, b, c and d AAD/2008/6/27; AAD/2008/6/28; AAD/2008/6/7

Watercolour sketch of lace detail (1904), watercolour sketch of lace used in a skirt of an ensemble (1904), a pencil drawing of a petticoat (*c.*1910–13) and lace used in a skirt (*c.*1910–13). This pictorial story demonstrates the creation and employment of lace throughout Lucile's *oeuvre*. The lace first appears as decorative embellishment to a skirt in 1904 then is updated and used in a drawing of a petticoat and replicated on a skirt.

Fig. 11 AAD/2008/6/28

Taken in a room designed by Elsie de Wolfe, this photograph pictures Lucile's New York staff, 1912–15. Mannequin Phyllis is seated in the last chair on right, and Gamela is second from the left, standing in the back row amongst other Lucile employees, who are immaculately dressed in their uniforms.

Fig. 12 AAD/2008/6/34

Lucile staged a *tableau vivant* to raise funds for the war orphans of France, in New York's Plaza Hotel in 1916. This was the first of many charity events that Lucile became involved with during and after World War I.

Fig. 13 AAD/2008/6/28

Part of Lucile's marketing strategy was to invite her house clients into interiors that resembled luxurious private residences to make them feel at home. This photograph shows a client having a toile fitted with the head of tailoring in such a room in the Paris house, *c.*1911–13. In the far corner a dressing table and mirror sit next to the marble fireplace with a large mirror above it. Beyond the table are various framed pictures hung one above another, giving the space a personal, 'lived in' touch.

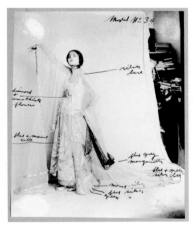

Fig. 14 AAD/2008/6/40

This photograph, from the album *Models, Spring 1918, New York*, shows Lucile's design studio at 160 Fifth Avenue, New York, was also used as a photography studio to document each season's models worn by her famous mannequins. Arjamand, Lucile's tall and slender New York mannequin, stands in front of a white curtain that was draped in the middle of the studio in front of shelves with books and albums stacked high. Hand-written annotations were added to the photograph to record model number (34), colour of fabric and trimmings.

Fig. 16 AAD/2008/6/42
Fashionable costume in Edwardian
theatrical productions became ever
more important to the success of plays,
and the women's press commented in
great detail on theatrical fashions. Lucile
designed costumes for the musical
The Catch of the Season at the Vaudeville
Theatre in 1904, using the commission
for publicity purposes and arranging a
mannequin parade at her couture house
prior to the opening. This branded
programme was given to guests invited
to the private view. It published a list of
acts and characters' names, and included
an essay expounding upon the beauty
and originality of the Lucile designs.

Fig. 19 AAD/2008/6/11
Lucile designed costumes for numerous
plays and films throughout her career.
This unused costume sketch for Miss
Yvonne Arnaud (1890–1958), a French
actress and founder of the Arnaud
Theatre, Guildford, was for an unknown
production and gives descriptions of
colour, fabric and accessories, as well
as a view of the back of the gown
(c.1912–15). It incorporates Lucile's
signature use of silk flowers and layers
of colourful chiffon over a flesh-toned
petticoat.

Fig. 17 AAD/2008/6/1
This sketch of a 'very smart afternoon'
ensemble, entitled 'Valgovina's Song in
the Spring', appeared in Lucile Ltd's
sketchbook and mannequin parade of
1904, and it was suggested that it should
be 'for Ascot and Garden Parties'.
The fanciful gigot sleeve and nipped-in
waist with long flared skirt is typical of
Edwardian fashion at this period, and
was entirely appropriate for spring and
summer parties. Many sketches and
prints bear the price of the ensemble
depicted – in this case 40 guineas.
Thus, the Archive gives a valuable
overview of the cost of Lucile garments
over a period of some 25 years.

Fig. 20 AAD/2008/6/38
Lucile began her long contract
designing for the *Ziegfeld Follies* in 1915,
for the original *Midnight Frolic*, a late-
night entertainment staged at New
York's New Amsterdam's rooftop
theatre. This show featured a glass
runway that let the *Follies* girls parade
over the audience's heads. The 'Poppy'
ensemble, modelled by Phyllis for the
'Flower' chiffon scene from the 1917
Follies, captures the poppy, with its large,
curved petals made into a headdress,
echoed in the costume's peplum.

Fig. 18 AAD/2008/6/42
This programme of dresses and hats made by Lucile in Paris for the Fall Season,
New York, 1913, demonstrates how significant Parisian design and association with
Paris was to New York and Lucile Ltd – it specifically states that the dresses and hats
were made by Lucile in *Paris*. As Lucile observed in her autobiography (pp.213–14):
'Without the lead of Paris, New York was lost sartorially.' Lucile exploited her
knowledge of Paris and its fashions to great advantage. She understood the importance
of beautifully designed interiors and (as the programme indicates) enlisted her good
friend and leading interior decorator Elsie de Wolfe to design her salons.

Fig. 21 AAD/2008/6/28
Lucile's sultry mannequin Gamela poses
in the garden of the Paris house. Filmy
silk is draped over her head, encircles her
body and is swathed around her ankles:
it veils a high-waisted dress with cross-
over bodice and tasselled decoration.
This look draws upon a multiplicity
of clothing references from around the
world and feeds into the prevailing
vogue for oriental styling.

Fig. 22 AAD/2008/6/4
Lucile designed many stage costumes
for Lily Elsie throughout her career.
This pencil drawing, annotated '1st dress,
Second Act without Coat, March 1910',
is almost certainly a design for the
operetta *The Count of Luxembourg*,
which was staged at Daly's Theatre in
May 1911. This pale pink silk chiffon
dress with a pale blue soft silk satin sash
at the waist and a pale blue flower at the
neckline, with ribbon trim, reveals
Lucile's understanding of the shades that
most suited Lily Elsie's blonde beauty.

Fig. 23 AAD/2008/6/12
Four hat designs, *c.*1915. Lucile's accessories formed essential and distinctive finishing touches to each ensemble. She wrote in her autobiography (p.79): 'In addition to the dresses themselves I used to show hats, shoes and gloves to harmonize with them, and even jewels.'

Fig. 24 AAD/2008/6/42
'The New Art of Woman Being the Expression of Personality in Curves and Colours' by 'The Saunterer', the magazine's society columnist, was a reprint of the article 'The New Art of Woman' from *The Smart Set*, May 1904. This was the journalist's response to Lucile's mannequin parade held on 28 April 1904, in her Hanover Square premises. The article provided excellent publicity for the house and the emphasis upon the art of dress must have gratified Lucile.

Fig. 25 AAD/2008/6/37
Lucile's vaudeville act *Fleurette's Dream at Péronne* was performed to benefit the Secours Franco-Americain pour la France Dévastée. She recalled in her autobiography (p.233): '…round the theme of the little mannequin dreaming in her cellar, I wove a pantomime consisting of a prologue and eight scenes, set to music.' The act was performed at the Booth Theatre in New York on 18 and 19 October 1917; it then toured with the B.F. Keith vaudeville circuit for ten weeks.

Fig. 27 AAD/2008/6/27
For the dancer Florence Walton, a famous client, Lucile created relatively short and full skirts to enable her to move with freedom, which were illustrated in Lucile's column in *Harper's Bazaar* for May 1916. This frothy concoction, photographed in 1917, might have been worn at Chez Maurice, the dance club that her husband and dance partner Maurice Mouve opened in New York.

Fig. 28 AAD/2008/6/12
Lucile only occasionally designed fashionable clothing for young girls and this pencil drawing of a demure, apron-fronted dress, *c.*1916, is a rare example. French couturier Jeanne Lanvin was famous for creating similar 'mother and daughter gowns', but this was not characteristic of Lucile's repertoire. The other examples of designs for children's clothing in the Lucile Archive were costumes for charitable events and a bridesmaid's ensemble for Miss Tompson's wedding.

Fig. 26 AAD/2008/6/8
This design, *c.*1913–15, specially commissioned for Mrs James Arthur, a New York socialite, gives precise details of materials, how the sleeve was to be crafted, as well as showing a sketch of the back of the ensemble, and how the coat would appear unbuttoned. Although signed 'Lucile', this design is possibly by Molyneux, resembling his streamlined approach to tailoring and and has annotations in the style of his handwriting.

Lucile in Other British Collections

This Appendix focuses on clothing and accessories by Lucile as well as Lucile design albums (which have samples of fabrics and trimmings attached) housed in British collections. The V&A collects fashion that leads (on an international basis) and the Museum of London aquires clothes that reflect life and society in London. These two museums have the major collections of Lucile in the UK. Other important dress collections at Bath and Brighton also have pieces by Lucile. We thank Curators Beatrice Behlen (Museum of London); Rosemary Harden and Eleanor Summers (Bath) and Eleanor Thompson (Brighton).

THE FURNITURE, TEXTILES AND FASHION DEPARTMENT AT THE V&A

FASHION ALBUMS

From Lucile Ltd. Autumn 1904 and *Autumn 1905* contain many textiles and trimmings, and are thus kept as part of the Furniture, Textiles and Fashion Collection at the V&A. The 1905 album (T.89a–1986) is fully described and faithfully replicated in this book.
From Lucile Ltd. Autumn 1904, 23, Hanover Square, London, W. (T.89–1986, purchased in auction with the later album) has 48 watercolour designs, probably by the fashion artist who worked on the Autumn 1905 album. Lucile's designs are mounted in an album of fragile, brittle, discoloured pages with a high acid content. Fabric samples and trimmings are crudely stitched through each page, creating weak points and encouraging the paper to crack. The Edwardian 'pouter pigeon' profile with mono-bosom pushed forward, minute waist and posterior thrust back, dominates the presentation of the ensembles, and designs range from tailored day wear to lavish evening attire in an array of 'Lucile colours'. The Autumn 1904 collection features a number of fanciful hats with wide or fly-away brims, veils and elaborate trimmings. Fabric snippets are in appealing abundance, and are roughly assembled, in comparison with their neater, pasted-in, 1905 counterparts. Seven ensembles have signature Lucile titles: 'Resignation' is a black evening gown; 'The Liquid Whisper of Spring' is a pale, leaf-green taffeta evening dress, while 'Venus' is a pale blue and pink dinner gown. In Lucile's hand-writing, five outfits (possibly for the stage) are inscribed 'Mrs Brown Potter' (the actress, an American red-head). Four of them are named: 'Passion's Thrall', 'Consolable Sorrow', 'The Legend of the Daisy' and 'The Awakening of Hope'. There is another, untitled, theatrical green ensemble of gown and cape. Although the 48 tiny fashionable figures and the complexities of their attire were carefully depicted in 1904, a year later the 69 designs for Autumn 1905 are more refined, revealing a confident, highly accomplished fashion artist.

FASHIONABLE DRESS

The Heather Firbank Collection
In 1960 the V&A acquired, and exhibited, a large collection of fashionable clothes worn by Miss Heather Firbank (1888–1954), daughter of the affluent MP, Sir Thomas Firbank, and sister of Ronald, the romantic novelist. Heather Firbank was dark-haired and slender: she was described in *The Times* as 'calmly exquisite' (30 September 1962), an expression that could also be applied to her taste in dress. Miss Firbank ordered her clothes from London's most exclusive London dressmakers, among them Lucile – if she especially liked something (according to *The Times*), she ordered it by the dozen. Extravagant and indulgent, she nonetheless cherished her elegant clothes and in 1921 meticulously packed away in storage trunks items she had purchased since 1908 and no longer wore, along with receipts and cuttings from ladies' magazines and newspapers. Heather Firbank favoured simple lines (she avoided extreme statements) and delicate colours, especially muted shades in the purple spectrum that complemented her name. Whilst her taste might have been restrained, her expenditure was not: her brother noted, in October 1924, that he 'assisted her in the payment of an overdue bill of £40 owed to her dressmaker, Lucile.'[1] Her gowns and accessories, custom-made for her by Lucile, include examples of tailored day wear; a dinner dress; and evening dress and accessories, c.1908–21. The V&A collection includes (in Museum number sequence):

Costume of black gabardine comprising coat and skirt, 1914–15 (T.27– & T.27a–1960)

Costume of grey mohair with velvet trimmings comprising jacket and skirt, c.1911–13 (T.36– & T.36a–1960)

Costume of dark grey worsted wool with matching bands and buttons, 1912–14 (the blouse and hat are not by Lucile) (T.38– & T.38a–1960)
(see opposite, top)

Diametrically opposed to Lucile decorative creations, with their romantic aura, are these austerely tailored works, which have a no-nonsense, clean-edged look – they were practical, often severe, and have a modern appeal. To soften the lines, such refined tailoring often incorporated subtle detailing, including self-fabric bands or tabs, and covered buttons. Used to accent this ensemble, they indicate the influence of military uniforms. This fine worsted ensemble would have been worn in town during the autumn and winter months. In a typically Lucile flourish and in contrast to the understated exterior, the costume is lined in satin with bold black and white stripes.

Evening gown of ivory-coloured silk charmeuse and chiffon, black silk velvet and machine-made lace, 1913 (T.31–1960), previously dated 1912–13. We are grateful to Randy Bigham for confirmation that the gown dates from 1913, and for providing references to photographs of it in *Vogue*, 13 May 1913, and *Vanity Fair*, April 1914 (worn by the dancer Lydia Kyasht, 1885–1959). *(see opposite, second image)*

By this date, the house was renowned for high-waisted designs with flowing, long, slender skirts that flattered most female bodies, giving an impression of height and streamlining the hips.

Showing Lucile's mastery of cut, the slit skirt (in pliant charmeuse) is cut in one panel with a single seam – it is draped asymmetrically at the front to give the impression of an overskirt. The deep, ultra-soft black silk velvet cummerbund has streamers that trail down the side, exaggerating the gown's lean lines.

Costume of brown silk, comprising jacket and skirt, c.1913 (T.41a–1960)

Dinner gown of black silk crêpe, 1912–13 (T.45–1960) *(see opposite, below)*

Lucile was famous for asymmetrical styles, of which this dress is an eloquent example. Set into a high waist, the bias-cut skirt is softly swathed over the left hip and is, in contrast, drawn tight to accentuate the curve of the right hip. The dress has long, narrow, ruched sleeves trimmed with cream silk. This is echoed around the low V neckline, which has a black lace 'modesty' inset. The hem extends to form a triangular hem. A photograph of a later, closely related gown appears in the Lucile archive 'Photographs of Models Autumn 1917, New York' (no. 51).

Day dress of black velveteen, trimmed with brown skunk fur, 1915 (T.49–1960)

Costume of blue gabardine comprising dress and jacket, 1914 (T.50– & 50a–1960)

Blouse of black silk chiffon with blue fabric flower decoration, c.1915 (T.60–1960)

Garter of black silk satin with three-dimensional fruits made in pink and purple satin (T.61–1960)

Hat, straw, with floral decoration, c.1921 (T.113–1960)

Hat, straw, with cream silk band, c.1908–10 (T.117–1960)

Acquired by Cecil Beaton for the Exhibition 'Fashion: An Anthology', 1971

'Fashion: An Anthology,' staged by Cecil Beaton, was the first major exhibition of modern fashion held at the V&A. At the time, Beaton stressed: 'I am so keen that when this display is shown it will convey a feeling of elegance and romanticism that the dresses pervaded in their own epochs.'[2] Subsequently many of the items were acquired by the Museum, including a pink cape that certainly fulfils Beaton's criteria.

Cloak, pink silk velvet, c.1915 (T.298–1974)

A caped evening cloak of rose-pink silk velvet with a devoré trailing rose design. Applied to the high gathered neckline are six small silk satin rosebuds, with three larger blooms at the back neckline. The cloak is double-layered, with an outer cloak that falls in fluid folds from the shoulders to form a broadly scalloped hem at hip-level. There is no label, but it is almost certainly by Lucile. Given by Mr Vern Lambert.

It was Vern Lambert, an Australian fashion historian and stylist who wore, collected and dealt in historical dress, who introduced fashion guru Anna Piaggi to 'vintage' clothes. She recalls accompanying him on his searches for rare, exquisite, fashionable historical clothes: 'We would go from country house to country house, and these women would go to their drawers and rustle around and then come out with these amazing dresses – Schiaparelli, Fortuny, Poiret – and they would be perfectly preserved because of the cold. Sometimes they were unworn and Vern would buy them and they were things of great beauty.'[3]

Also by Lucile

'Carresaute', evening dress of blue silk with lace and rouleaux trimmings, comprising bodice and skirt, Autumn 1905 (photographed and described on pp.176–181). (T.42:1 & 2–2007)

Dress of purple and green silk with applied vine decoration, c.1908. Probably fancy dress or theatrical costume for a Bacchante. Adern Holt, in *Fancy Dresses Described*, in print from 1879 for over 15 years, recommended a dress (for a 'worshipper of Bacchus') of apple green silk, the draperies caught up with white and purple grapes. (T.557–1993)

Boudoir cap of pink silk trimmed with gold and silver lace, c.1919. (T.3–1961)

Wedding ensemble comprising a dress, veil, train, petticoat and three garters c.1922. Charmeuse and tulle with metal strip embroidery and pearl edging on the veil. (T314-F. 1985).

Hat, cap of white machine-embroidered tulle with fabric flowers, c.1922. (T.65–1966)

LUCILE LTD IN OTHER BRITISH COLLECTIONS

THE MUSEUM OF LONDON

In a letter written to the Curator (22 May 1928) Lucile offered to donate to the Museum collection some of the dresses shown in her first parade in Paris in 1911. She informed him that she had personally preserved these particular garments because they had a 'certain sentimental interest' and indicated that the models had been made for Lily Elsie and Gertie Millar. Addressing the Museum's London-specific collection policy, she advised that 'They were made in London by London girls…' (and continues as quoted in the Introduction, p.14). The Museum acquired two dresses: one in eggshell-green silk georgette created for Lily Elsie in 1910, the other of blue satin and embroidered with georgette, for Gertie Millar to wear in *The Quaker Girl* (1911).

A coat of grey face-cloth embroidered with white silk cord, c.1910

A purple silk velvet and gold lamé opera coat with decorative tassels, lined in turquoise silk satin, c.1911.

A costume comprising a skirt and jacket in black herringbone wool suiting lined with purple silk satin, worn by Heather Firbank, c.1914.

A court dress of pale pink silk satin with tan-coloured tulle sleeves and beaded embroidery around the waist and two beaded tassels; train; fan and dress panel, 1922.

Thirty-one hand coloured fashion plates, some mounted with fabric samples attached, early 20th century.

THE FASHION MUSEUM, BATH

A wedding dress, 1907

A cream and black wool day dress, 1908

A blue and gold silk dress with beading and embroidery, 1911

A pink, cream and silver silk evening dress with metal thread embroidery, c.1910

A wedding dress, 1911

A blouse of dark blue silk satin, c.1912

A blouse of cream-coloured silk chiffon with lace, c.1912

A blouse of blue and cream-coloured silk chiffon with lace, c.1912

BRIGHTON MUSEUM AND ART GALLERY

A two-piece tailored costume of dark brown silk with fur lapels and cuffs. The jacket has a diagonal hem. It was ordered and worn by Maud Messel, c.1912-13

Lucile in American Collections

The Fashion Institute of Technology houses the largest paper collection of Lucile's designs in America and the University of California, Los Angeles, has a noteworthy collection. The Chicago History Museum, The Metropolitan Museum of Art Costume Institute, New York, the Kent State Museum in Ohio, as well as Philadelphia, hold beautiful examples of fashionable dress and accessories from Lucile's American and European establishments.

The most significant American paper collection of Lucile's designs is housed in the Fashion Institute of Technology's Gladys Marcus Library, Special Collections, New York, and spans the period 1915–25. This collection comprises 923 watercolour sketches and 2,415 photographs and press clippings, which document Lucile's career as a dressmaker and theatrical costumier. The collection focuses upon her New York output, but there are also some items from Chicago, London and Paris. The Museum at the FIT houses two evening gowns and an ecru lace and velvet 'dressy' afternoon suit. The suit and a number of paper designs (supplemented with items from private collectors) were displayed in the exhibition 'Designing the It Girl: Lucile and Her Style' in 2005. Also in New York, the Museum of the City of New York included performance costumes by Lucile Ltd in the exhibition 'Broadway Costumes: Fit to be Danced In' (1999–2000), which was organized by Phyllis Magidson and Barbara Straytner.

The other major paper collection forms part of the University of California, Los Angeles's Libraries Department of Special Collections. There are 255 coloured fashion sketches with pen or pencil descriptions boxed and arranged chronologically from 1913 to 1925. Most of the material relates to the period when Lucile lived and worked in the States.

Several institutional dress collections throughout America possess garments bearing the Lucile label, and these include the Kent State Museum in Ohio, the Chicago History Museum, Illinois, the Philadelphia Museum of Art, Pennsylvania, and the Costume Institute at the Metropolitan Museum of Art, New York. The Chicago History Museum collection dates from 1913 to the 1920s: it houses rare, surviving examples of garments ordered from Lucile's Chicago establishment, such as wedding gowns, bridesmaid's gowns, evening dresses and hats, as well as a 1920s black silk coat with multicoloured embroidery from the Paris house, and a gown worn by Irene Castle in Irving Berlin's *Watch Your Step*. The Costume and Textiles collections in the Philadelphia Museum of Art hold seven Lucile items: a hat, a bodice and five dresses. One of these was named 'Happiness' (1916); another is a beautiful, ivory-coloured, peg-top-wired, peplum silk taffeta and silver net dress trimmed with silver lace, chartreuse-yellow satin and beaded flowers. The Kent State University Museum has five dresses and one hat dating from 1915 to 1920, which showcase Lucile's mastery of colour and feminine flourishes. An example of this is an evening dress of 1920 in apricot and lavender silk with silver lace, with a turquoise silk cord-trimmed chemise that has a cummerbund bodice of faille and narrow oversashes of lavender, turquoise and chartreuse-yellow silks, together with another sash of Wedgwood-blue chiffon tied with a knot drapes with two frills. After the V&A collection, it is the Metropolitan Museum of Art Costume Institute's collection that has the largest quantity of Lucile garments. Dating from 1913 to the 1920s, there are evening dresses, afternoon ensembles, a dinner and wedding dress, dance dresses and one hat.

Glossary

The vocabulary of fashion is ever-changing – these terms (some with long histories) were current at end of the nineteenth century and in the early 1900s. Many are now obsolete, while others have subtly altered meanings.

barège Fine, gauze-like fabric of wool combined with cotton or silk. Originally made in Barèges, France.

basque Usually a short, gently flared extension of the bodice below the waist. French for the skirt of a coat or jacket.

bertha Deep, falling collar, sometimes attached to a low neckline

bone channel Narrow band of fabric applied within a bodice or corset, into which a stiffening strip of whalebone or steel is inserted

bouquet de corsage Cluster of real or artificial flowers attached to a bodice (corsage). Has become shortened to 'corsage'.

cascade Flounce or ruffle, often of lace. It is fastened at the neck and cascades down the centre front.

challis Lightweight woven worsted and silk

charmeuse Lightweight, pliable satin-faced fabric with low lustre, much used for draped gowns

chemisette A modesty 'fill in', worn under a low-necked bodice, usually of fine white fabric or lace

chiné Fabric with a warp that is printed, painted or dyed before weaving with a plain weft, giving a blurred, misty pattern. French for 'variegated'.

dicky/dickey Blouse or shirt front, often decorative, usually detachable

échelle Vertical row of decorative motifs (usually ribbon bows). French for 'ladder'.

entre-deux Narrow insertion of lace or embroidery joining two panels of fabric, much used in de luxe lingerie and blouses.

éolienne Lightweight woven fabric of silk and worsted or silk and cotton. The weft is heavier than the warp, giving a horizontal corded texture.

faced cloth, face cloth, cloth High-quality, dense but pliable, medium-weight wool with a low-lustre surface

fichu Draped scarf or shawl (usually of white, delicate material) worn around the neck and shoulders, and tied or crossed over at the breast. French for 'neckerchief'.

garçonne Term used to describe the style of dress worn by fashionable women in the 1920s. It is believed to have originated with Victor Margueritte's novel *La Garçonne* (1922) whose scandalous young heroine cut her hair short and wore masculine style clothes. The term 'flapper' is often used interchangeably.

gigot/leg of mutton Sleeve with a very full upper part (at the shoulder) which then narrows to a tight fit over the forearms and at the wrist. So called because of its resemblance to this particular joint of meat.

jabot Longish frill or ruffle, often of lace, fastened around the neck, which hangs down the bodice centrefront. From the French for 'frill' (of a shirt or dress).

mousseline de soie Opaque silk muslin with a firm finish. French for 'chiffon'.

passementerie Mainly glossy braids, fringes, tassels, embroideries and cords. French for 'trimmings'.

peignoir 'At home' jacket or robe. French for 'dressing gown', from *'peign'* ('comb').

pèlerine Short cape with long pendant ends. French for 'cape'.

peplum Overskirt or extension (varied in length and style) of the upper part of a garment, attached at the waist. The term can be traced back to the costume of Ancient Greece.

plastron Front panel of a bodice. French for 'breastplate', or 'shirt front'.

plush Fabric, usually wool, with a long, lustrous pile

pneumonia blouse Low-neck blouse (usually a V neck) in lightweight fabric, so called as it exposed the chest and throat, thereby encouraging colds.

Pompadour Eighteenth-century style of dress, fabrics, accessories and coiffure, etc., associated with Madame de Pompadour (the Marquise de Pompadour, 1721–1764), mistress of Louis XV.

princess line/*en princesse* Garment without a waist seam. A princess gown has a bodice and skirt (usually slightly flared), cut in one. It is associated with Alexandra when she was Princess of Wales.

rabat Detachable band collar, often in lace with pendant fall(s).

redingote Tailored, outdoor coat or long jacket, fitted or semi-fitted and up to ⅞ length. A French corruption of the English 'riding coat'.

rouleau(x) Very narrow tubular piping of bias-cut fabric, sometimes with an internal cord for firmness. Used for applied decoration and edgings, as it can be manipulated into intricate patterns. French for 'roll'.

saque Loose, unfitted, sometimes voluminous garment that flares from shoulder to hem without a waist. Adapted from the word *'sac'* (French for 'sack').

saut de lit Morning dressing gown (light kimonos were popular), to wear on getting out of bed.

sautoir Long string of pearls or chain

sortie de bal Usually ornate evening cloak or coat (often of loose cut), worn over ball gowns

soutache Narrow, decorative braid. French, from the Hungarian *'szuszak'*. Also known as 'Russian braid'.

tablier Apron-like front part of a garment. French for 'apron'.

toque Usually a flattish, small hat without a brim.

Zouave Short, collarless, bolero-like jacket, usually with curved fronts, fastened only at the neck and often decorated with applied braid. An adaptation of the jackets worn by Algerian Zouave troops.

Chronology

1863

Lucy Christiana Sutherland is born in London

1884

Marries James Charles Stuart Wallace (her senior by 18 years)

1885

Daughter Esmé is born

1891

Census: L.C. Wallace (25) (*sic*) at 25 Davies Street, Berkeley Square, London, with mother, Eleanor Kennedy (50), husband James C.S. Wallace (46), and Esmé Wallace (5), with four servants.

1893

Lucy Christiana Wallace petitions for a divorce; decree absolute granted 1895

She stated that she started her business as a dressmaker and adopts the trade name 'Lucile' (Lady Duff Gordon, in 1922)

1894

Court directory, 'Mrs Wallace, 25 Davies Street, Berkley Square, London'. Dresses the Countess of Warwick for presentation at court.

1895

Designs costumes for sister Elinor Glyn and Mrs Willie James to wear in an amateur production, *Diplomacy*.

Commercial directory, 'Mrs Lucy Wallace, court dressmaker, 24 Old Burlington Street'. This seems to be her first appearance as a dressmaker in a London directory.

1896, 1897

Directories, 'Mrs Lucy Wallace, court dressmaker, 24 Old Burlington Street'

1897

Street directory, '25 Davies Street, Mrs Wallace, Mrs David Kennedy'

First professional costumes for Henry Arthur Jones's play *The Liars*, produced by Charles Wyndham and starring Mary Moore and Irene Vanbrugh

1898–1901

Directories, '17 Hanover Square, Mrs Lucy Wallace, dressmaker and court dressmaker'

1900 MAY

Marries Sir Cosmo Edmund Duff Gordon at the British Consulate in Venice

1902

'Madame Lucile, 17 Hanover Square' appears in directories

1903

'Madame Lucile/Lucile' is not listed in the London Post Office directories

She stated that she sold her business to Lucile Ltd (Lady Duff Gordon, 1922). The Board includes Sir Cosmo. She remains a director and dress designer to this company.

1904

Lucile London Ltd is incorporated

Trades directory, 'Dressmakers, Lucile Limited, 23 Hanover Square, London'

Mannequin parade is staged at Lucile Ltd, 23 Hanover Square, a private view entitled 'Costume Suggestions: Being Studies in the Expression of Personality in Curves and Colours'.

1905, 1907

Commercial directory, 'Lucile Lim. and Lucile Ltd court dressmakers, 23 Hanover Square, London'

1907

Designs costumes for Lily Elsie in London stage debut of Franz Lehár's *The Merry Widow* (produced by George Edwardes at Daly's Theatre).

1909

This year is described as the zenith of the London business in her autobiography (p.121). Around this time she is making £40,000 a year.

1910

Writes weekly column for the *New York American Examiner*, a Hearst paper

Opens New York branch at 17 West 36th Street

Edward Molyneux begins working for Lucile Ltd as a sketch artist

DECEMBER
Lucile Ltd, Paris, is incorporated with a nominal capital of £25,100. First directors are Lucy Christiana Duff Gordon, Cosmo Duff Gordon and Algernon Osmond Miles.

1911

FEBRUARY
Lucile Ltd, New York, is incorporated, with a nominal capital of £9,100. First directors are Lucy Christiana Duff Gordon, Cosmo Duff Gordon and Algernon Osmond Miles.

The New York house is sued by the U.S. Treasury Department for conspiracy to defraud the government by falsifying customs invoices on European imports. Charges are dropped, but the house is fined for managerial negligence.

APRIL
Paris branch is inaugurated at 11 rue de Penthièvre with a fashion parade

1912

APRIL
Sir Cosmo and Lady Duff-Gordon survive the sinking of *The Titanic*

MAY
The couple attend the Court of Inquiry, London, following the sinking

AUGUST
Writes first article for *Good Housekeeping*, column entitled 'Her Wardrobe'

Transfers New York premises to 37–39 West 57th Street

Buys Pavillon Mars in Versailles

1913

Designs first film costumes, for Alice Joyce in *The American Princess*

1913–1922

Writes correspondence columns for American *Harper's Bazaar*

1914

Moves from Paris to New York. Works from a design studio at 160 Fifth Avenue, and leases an apartment on Central Park South.

Provides Billie Burke with wedding trousseau for her marriage to Florenz Ziegfeld

1915

Opens Chicago branch at 1400 Lake Shore Drive

Designs first costumes for the *Ziegfeld Follies* and *Midnight Frolic*

Dresses Irene Castle in *The Whirl of Life*, and supplies gowns for the film's fashion parade sequence, which takes place in a salon designed to replicate Lucile's New York premises

1915–19

Teaches at the New York School of Fine and Applied Art (later renamed 'Parsons School of Design')

APRIL
Signs contract with Otis F. Wood, top New York advertising agent, giving him the exclusive right to market garments and other products bearing her endorsement for one year

1915

Sir Cosmo Duff Gordon files for a privately settled legal separation

1916

Appoints spokesperson and fundraising coordinator for the Orphelinat des Armées, and organizes *Chansons Vivantes* in aid of the orphanage, which runs for a week at the Plaza Hotel, New York

1916, 1921 and 1926 Edward Molyneux is listed as a shareholder in Lucile Ltd, Paris

Moves into shorefront estate, 'The Anchorage', at Mamaroneck-on-the-Sound, Long Island

1916–17

Designs ready-to-wear collections for Sears, Roebuck and Co. catalogue

1917

Wood v. Lucy, Lady Duff Gordon. Wood wins, Lucile found in breach of contract.

Tours the vaudeville circuit with her fashion revue, *Fleurette's Dream at Péronne* in aid of the charity Secours Franco-Americain pour la France Devastée, contracted with Keith Vaudeville Circuit to tour major East Coast cities for a ten-week run.

Designs interiors for limousines and town cars for the Chalmers Motor Co. (later the Chrysler Corporation)

1919

MAY

Lucile appoints wholesale manufacturer Otto Bernard Shulhof as her attorney and agent for the four companies that comprises Lucile Ltd, and additionally appoints him a Director (described as 'Director of Lucile Limited, London, Paris, New York and Chicago and Principal of Shulhof & Co., New York in Company Records). Lucile sells stock and becomes a salaried designer

Position in New York becomes untenable, returns to London, and then moves to Paris

Dismisses Molyneux, who opens his own house in November at 14 rue Royale

Lucile Ltd, London, begins winding-up process. Records for the London company are destroyed in 1967 (date confirmed by Companies House).

At this time the earnings from her four companies amount to about £10,000 a year

1921

Lucile Ltd moves New York premises to 19 and 21 East 54th Street and Madison Avenue

Writes first weekly column for *The London Daily Sketch*, which has a companion page in the *Illustrated Sunday Herald* until 1927

Chicago branch closes

1922

Designs last costumes for *Ziegfeld Follies*

Lady Duff Gordon is 'dismissed' from Lucile Ltd, Paris

Lucile Ltd, New York, declared bankrupt

OCTOBER

Lady Duff Gordon declared bankrupt in London, proceedings start and are completed in April 1923. Otto B. Shulhof takes control of Lucile Ltd, Paris, dismisses Lucile and sues her for recovery of stolen company money. Lucile counter-sues for wrongful dismissal. Both cases are dropped.

Lucile Ltd, New York bought by J.M. Giddings & Co.

1923

Moves back to London after selling property in France, and operates from Rossetti Gardens Mansions as Lady or Lucy Duff Gordon Ltd

Lucile Ltd, London, shows first collection without Lucile as chief designer

1924

Lucile Ltd, London, closes

1927–28

Lucile teaches in New York at Cooper Union and Trapenhagen School of Fashion

1928

Writes last *London Daily Sketch* columns

12 APRIL

Lucy Duff Gordon Limited is incorporated with a nominal capital of £4,000. Premises at 120 New Bond Street.

1930

Lucile Ltd, Paris finally dissolved in February. Lucy Duff Gordon Limited begins voluntary winding-up process in October and completes in August 1932

Writes three articles for *Weldon's Ladies' Journal*

1931

APRIL

Sir Cosmo Duff Gordon dies

1932

OCTOBER

Lucile Ltd, New York, is finally dissolved

Publication of her autobiography *Discretions and Indiscretions*

1933

Writes her final article for *The Saturday Review*

1935

20 APRIL

Lady Duff Gordon dies in a London nursing home

22 APRIL

Obituaries published in *The Times* and *The New York Times*

25 APRIL

Funeral of Lady Duff Gordon. She is buried at Brookwood Cemetery, London.

Bibliography

Of particular relevance to Lady Duff
Gordon and Lucile Ltd:

Duff Gordon, Lady Lucy, *Discretions and
Indiscretions* (London, 1932)

Etherington-Smith, Meredith,
and Pilcher, Jeremy, *The IT Girls:
Elinor Glyn and Lucy, Lady Duff Gordon*
(London, 1986)

Fashion Institute of Technology,
Designing the It Girl: Lucile and Her Style
(New York, 2005)

Glyn, Anthony, *Elinor Glyn*
(London, 1955)

Glyn, Elinor, *A Romantic Adventure*
(London, 1936)

*Portfolio of Lady Duff Gordon's Original
Designs: Wearing Apparel for the Women
of America* (Chicago, Summer and
Spring 1917)

Richardsons' Crochet Library, *The Lady
Duff Gordon Series, no. 16 Crochet Yokes
and Blouses*; no. 17 *Crochet Edgings and
Insertions*; no. 18 *Irish and Cluny Crochet*,
no. 19 *Boudoir and Breakfast Caps*
(New York: Chicago, 1917)

*Weldon's Ladies' Journal (of Dress, Fashion,
Needlework, Literature and Art)*, London,
July 1930 (no. 613), August 1930 (no. 614),
September 1930 (no. 615)

Further reading

Ackroyd, Peter, *London: The Biography*
(London, 2000)

Adburgham, Alison, *Shops and Shopping
1800–1914* (London, 1964)

Adby, Jane, and Gere, Charlotte,
The Souls (London, 1984)

Alexandre, Arsène, *Les Reines de
l'aiguille. Modistes et Couturieres*
(Paris: Berlin, 1902)

Allen, Robert C., *Horrible Prettiness:
Burlesque and American Culture*
(Chapel Hill: London, 1991)

Andrews, Allen, *The Follies of King
Edward VII* (London, 1975)

Anon., *Comments of a Countess*
(London, 1901)

Arch, Nigel, and Marschner, Joanna,
Splendour at Court (London, 1987)

Aria, Mrs, *Costume, Fanciful, Historical
and Theatrical* (London, 1906)

Aronson, Theo, *The King in Love:
Edward VII's Mistresses* (London, 1988)

Asquith, Lady Cynthia, *Remember and
be Glad* (London, 1952)

Atfield, Judy, and Kirkham, Pat (eds),
*A View from the Interior: Feminism, Women
and Design* (London, 1989)

Auchincloss, Louis, *The Vanderbilt Era:
Profiles of a Gilded Age* (New York, 1990)

Audsley, George Ashdown, *Colour in
Dress* (London, 1912)

Balsan, Consuelo Vanderbilt, *The Glitter
and the Gold* (London, 1953)

Banner, Lois W., *American Beauty:
A Social History through Two Centuries of
the American Idea, Ideal, and Image of the
Beautiful Woman* (New York, 1983)

Battersea, Constance, Lady Rothschild,
Reminiscences (London, 1922)

Beaton, Cecil, *The Book of Beauty*
(London, 1930)

——, *The Glass of Fashion*
(London, 1954)

Beckson, Karl, *London in the 1890s:
A Cultural History* (New York:
London, 1992)

Beetham, Margaret, *A Magazine of
Her Own? Domesticity and Desire in
the Woman's Magazine, 1800–1914*
(London: New York, 1996)

Bennett, Helen, and Stevenson, Sara,
*Van Dyke in Checked Trousers. Fancy Dress
in Art and Life* (Edinburgh, 1978)

Benson, E.F., *As We Were* (London, 1932)

Bentley-Cranch, Dana, *Edward VII*
(London, 1992)

Bloom, Ursula, *The Elegant Edwardian*
(London, 1957)

Borgé, Jacques, and Viasnoff, Nicolas,
Archives de la Mode (Paris, 1995)

Brandon, Ruth, *The Dollar Princesses:
Sagas of Upward Mobility 1870–1914*
(New York, 1980)

Braun, Adolphe Armand, *Figures,
Faces and Folds* (London, 1928)

Breward, Christopher, and Evans,
Caroline (eds), *Fashion and Modernity*
(Oxford: New York, 2005)

Breward, Christopher, *Fashioning
London: Clothing and the Modern
Metropolis* (Oxford: New York, 2004)

Brown Potter, Cora, *Secrets of Beauty
and Mysteries of Health* (San Francisco:
New York, c.1910)

Buchan, Susan, Lady Tweedsmuir,
An Edwardian Lady (London, 1966)

Buckley, Cheryl, and Fawcett, Hilary,
*Fashioning the Feminine: Representation
and Women's Fashion from the Fin de Siècle
to the Present* (London: New York, 2002)

Burgess, Fred W., *The Practical Retail
Draper: A Complete Guide for the Drapery
and Allied Trades, vol.V* (London, 1912)

Caffrey, Kate, *The 1900s Lady*
(London, 1976)

Cannadine, David, *Decline and Fall of the
British Aristocracy* (New Haven, 1992)

——, *Aspects of Aristocracy*
(London, 1994)

Chadwick, Luie M., *Fashion Drawing
and Design* (London, 1926)

Chapon, François, *Mystère et splendeurs
de Jacques Doucet* (Paris, 1984)

Chase, Edna Woolman and Ilka, *Always
in Vogue* (London, 1954)

Coates, Tim, *Patsy: the Story of Mary
Cornwallis-West* (London, 2003)

Coleman, Elizabeth Ann, *The Opulent
Era: The Fashions of Worth, Doucet and
Pingat* (The Brooklyn Museum exhib.
cat., 1990)

Cooper, Diana, *The Rainbow Comes and
Goes* (London: Boston, 1958)

Cornwallis-West, George, *Edwardian
Hey-days* (London, 1930)

Cowles, Virginia, *Edward VII and his
Circle* (London, 1956)

Crawford, M.D.C., *The Ways of Fashion*
(New York, 1941)

Cunnington, C. Willett, *The Perfect Lady*
(London: New York, 1948)

De la Haye, Amy, and Mendes, Valerie,
Twentieth Century Fashion
(London, 1999)

De Laszló, Sandra, *A Brush with
Grandeur: Philip Alexius de Lazló*
(London, 2004)

De Marly, Diana, *The History of Haute
Couture 1850–1950* (London, 1980)

De Stoeckel, Baroness, *Not All Vanity*
(London, 1950)

De Wolfe, Elsie, *After All* (London, 1935)

Deslandres, Yvonne, *Paul Poiret 1879–1944*
(London, 1987)

Edes, Elisabeth (ed.), *The Age of
Extravagance* (London, 1956)

Eliot, Elizabeth, *They All Married Well*
(London, 1959)

Evans, Caroline, 'The Enchanted
Spectacle', *Fashion Theory: The Journal of
Dress, Body & Culture*, 5:3 (September
2001), pp.271–310

Ewing, Elizabeth, *History of Twentieth
Century Fashion* (London, 1986)

Forbes, Lady Angela (St Clair Erskine),
Memories and Base Details (London, 1922)

Forester, the Hon. Mrs C.W., *This Age of
Beauty* (London, 1935)

Garnier, Guillaume, *Paul Poiret et Nicole
Groult* (Musée de la Mode et du
Costume, Palais Galliera, Paris exhib.
cat., 1986)

Glenn, Susan Anita, *Female Spectacle:
The Theatrical Roots of Modern Feminism*
(Cambridge, Mass.: London 2000)

Glyn, Elinor, *The Visits of Elizabeth*
(London, 1901, first serialized in
The World)

——, *Elizabeth Visits America*
(London, 1909)

Greer, Howard, *Designing Male*
(New York, 1952)

Gregory, Alexis, *The Gilded Age:
The Super Rich of the Edwardian Era*
(London, 1993)

Hartnell, Norman, *Silver and Gold*
(London, 1954)

Hawes, Elizabeth, *Fashion is Spinach*
(New York, 1938)

Hayes, J.W., *The Draper and Haberdasher:
A Guide to the General Drapery Trade*
(London, 1878)

Higham, Charles, *The Duchess of
Windsor: The Secret Life* (New York, 1988)

Holt, Ardern, *Fancy Dresses Described*
(first published 1879), 6th edition
(London, 1896)

Homberger, Eric, *Mrs Astor's New York:
Money and Social Power in the Gilded Age*
(New Haven, Connecticut:
London, 2002)

Jachimowicz, Elizabeth, *Eight Chicago
Women and Their Fashions 1860–1929*
(Chicago, 1978)

Jullian, Philippe, *La Belle Epoque*
(Metropolitan Museum of Art
exhib. cat., 1982)

Kaplan, Joel H. and Stowell, Sheila,
Theatre and Fashion (Cambridge, 1995)

Keppel, Sonia, *Edwardian Daughter*
(London, 1958)

Kjellberg, Anne, and North, Susan,
*Style and Splendour: The Wardrobe of
Queen Maud of Norway* (London, 2005)

Koch, W. John, *Daisy Princess of Pless
1873–1943* (Edmonton, 2002)

Kwint, Marius, Breward, Christopher,
and Aynsley, Jeremy, *Material Memories:
Design & Evocation* (Oxford: New York,
1999)

Land, Andrew, *Motoring Costume*
(Princes Risborough, 1987)

Langley Moore, Doris, *Fashion Through
Fashion Plates* (London, 1971)

Lambert, Angela, *Unquiet Souls:
the Indian Summer of the British Aristocracy,
1880–1918* (London, 1984)

Langtry, Lillie, *The Days I Knew*
(London, 1925)

Laver, James, *Taste and Fashion*
(London, 1937)

——, *Edwardian Promenade*
(Cambridge, Mass., 1958)

——, *The Age of Optimism. Manners
and Morals 1848–1914* (London, 1966)

Leese, Elizabeth, *Costume Design in the
Movies* (Bembridge, 1976)

Leslie, Anita, *Edwardians in Love*
(New York, 1972)

Levitt, Sarah, *Fashion in Photographs
1880–1900* (London, 1991)

Lewis, Alfred A., *Ladies and Not-So-
Gentle-Women: Elizabeth Marbury,
Anne Morgan, Elsie de Wolfe,
Anne Vanderbilt, and Their Times*
(New York, 2000)

Lomax, James, and Ormond, Richard,
John Singer Sargent and the Edwardian Era
(Leeds, London and Detroit, 1979)

Longford, Elizabeth, *Louisa Lady in
Waiting* (London, 1979)

Lord, Walter, *A Night to Remember:
Illustrated Edition* (London, 1976)

Lynch, Don, *Titanic: An Illustrated History*
(London, 1992)

McKellar, Susie and Sparke, Penny (eds), *Interior Design and Identity* (Manchester, 2004)

McKibben, Ross, *Classes and Cultures England 1918–1951* (Oxford, 1998)

MacQueen-Pope, W., *Gaiety: Theatre of Enchantment* (London, 1949)

Marcus, Geoffrey, *The Maiden Voyage* (London, 1969)

A Member of the Aristocracy, *Manners and Rules of Good Society*, 26th edition (1902)

Mizejewski, Linda, *Ziegfeld Girl: Image and Icon in Culture and Cinema* (Durham: London, 1999)

Moore, Mary, *Charles Wyndham and Mary Moore* (Edinburgh, 1925)

Mordant Cook, J., *The Rise of the Nouveaux Riches: Style and Status in Victorian and Edwardian Architecture* (London, 1999)

Morgan, Anne, *The American Girl: Her Education. Her Responsibility, Her Recreation, Her Future* (New York, 1915)

Murphy, Sophia, *The Duchess of Devonshire's Ball* (London, 1984)

Nicolson, Nigel, *Mary Curzon* (London, 1977)

Nystrom, Paul, *Economics of Fashion* (New York, 1928)

O'Neill, Alistair, *London After a Fashion* (London, 2007)

Pearce, Susan M., *Interpreting Objects and Collections* (London, 1994)

Peel, Mrs C.S., *Life's Enchanted Cup* (London, 1933)

Pepper, Terence, *High Society Portraits 1897–1914* (London, 1998)

Pick, Michael, *Be Dazzled! Norman Hartnell. 60 Years of Glamour and Fashion* (New York, 2007)

Picken, Mary, *The Language of Fashion* (New York, 1939)

Picken, Mary, and Miller, Dora Loues, *Dressmakers of France* (New York, 1956)

Pless, Daisy, Princess, *Daisy Princess of Pless, by Herself* (London, 1929)

——, *More about Myself and Friends* (London, 1930)

——, *From My Private Diary* (London, 1931)

——, *What I Left Unsaid* (London, 1936)

Poiret, Paul, *My First Fifty Years* (London, 1931)

A Practical Guide for the Retails Clothier and Outfitter to all the Latest Methods of Successful Advertising (publicity, London, 1910)

Priestley, J.B., *The Edwardians* (London, 1970)

Pritchard, Mrs Eric, *The Cult of Chiffon* (London, 1902)

Quennell, Peter, and Sage, Lorna, *The Last Edwardians: An Illustrated History of Violet Trefusis and Alice Keppel* (Boston, 1985)

Rappaport, Erika Diane, *Shopping for Pleasure: Women in the Making of London's West End* (Princeton, 2000)

Raverat, Gwen, *Period Piece. A Cambridge Childhood* (London, 1952)

Reed, Christopher (ed.), *Not At Home: The Suppression of Domesticity in Modern Art and Architecture* (New York and London, 1996)

Rennolds Milbank, Caroline, *New York Fashion: The Evolution of American Style* (New York, 1989)

——, *Couture: The Great Designers* (London, 1985)

Ribeiro, Aileen, *Dress in Eighteenth Century Europe 1715–1789* (London, 1984)

——, *Dress and Morality* (London, 1986)

Roger-Milès, Léon, *Les Créateurs de la Mode* (Paris, 1910)

Rose, Jonathan, *The Edwardian Temperament: 1895–1919* (Athens, Ohio and London, 1986)

Rothstein, Natalie (ed.), *Four Hundred Years of Fashion* (London, 1984)

Ruffer, Jonathan Garnier, *The Big Shots: Edwardian Shooting Parties* (New York, 1977)

Sackville-West, Vita, *The Edwardians* (London, 1930)

Sawdon, Mary, *A History of Victorian Skirt Grips* (Cambridge, 1995)

Schwartz, Hillel, *The Culture of the Copy: Striking Likenesses, Unreasonable Facsimiles* (New York, 2000)

Sermoneta, Duchess of, *Things Past* (1929)

Sirop, Dominique, *Paquin* (Lyons, 1989)

Slattery-Christy, David, *The Life and Times of Lily Elsie: Anything But Merry* (Milton Keynes, 2008)

Sloane, Florence A., *Maverick in Mauve* (New York, 1983)

Souhami, Diana, *Mrs Keppel and her Daughter* (New York, 1996)

Sparke, Penny, *Elsie de Wolfe: The Birth of Modern Interior Decoration* (New York, 2005)

Splatt, Cynthia, *Isadora Duncan and Gordon Craig: The Prose & Poetry of Action* (San Francisco, 1988)

Sproule, Anna, *The Social Calendar* (Poole, 1978)

Stanley, Louis T., *The London Season* (London, 1955)

Steele, Valerie, *Fashion and Eroticism: Ideals of Feminine Beauty from the Victorian Era to the Jazz Age* (New York: Oxford, 1985)

Swanberg, S.A., *Citizen Hearst: A Biography of William Randolph Hearst* (New York, 1962)

Taylor, Lou, *The Study of Dress History* (Manchester, 2002)

——, *Establishing Dress History* (Manchester, 2004)

Tebbel, John, and Zuckerman, Mary Ellen, *The Magazine in America 1741–1990* (New York and Oxford, 1991)

Tebbel, John, *The Life and Good Times of William Randolph Hearst* (London, 1953)

Terriss, Ellaline, *Just a Little Bit of String* (London, 1955)

Thieme, Charles Otto, *Simply Stunning: 200 Years of Fashion from the Cincinnati Art Museum* (Cininnati, 1988)

Thompson, Paul, *The Edwardians: The Remaking of British Society*, (London, 1975)

Tickner, Lisa, *The Spectacle of Woman: Imagery of the Suffrage Campaign 1907–1914* (London, 1987)

Troubridge, Lady Laura, *Memories and Reflections* (London, 1925)

Troy, Nancy J., *Couture Culture* (Cambridge, Massachusetts and London, 2003)

Walkley, Christina, and Foster, Vanda, *Crinolines and Crimping Irons* (London, 1978)

Walkley, Christina, *Dressed to Impress: 1840–1914* (London, 1989)

Warwick, Frances, Countess of, *Life's Ebb and Flow* (London, 1929)

——, *Afterthoughts* (London, 1931)

Waugh, Norah, *The Cut of Women's Clothes* (London, 1968)

Wharton, Edith, *A Backward Glance* (New York, 1934)

White, Cynthia, *Women's Magazines* (London, 1970)

White, Palmer, *Poiret* (London, 1973)

Williams, Mrs Hwfa, *It was Such Fun* (London, 1935)

Williamson, Mrs F. Harcourt, *The Book of Beauty* (annually during the 1890s)

Winterburn, Florence Hull, *Principles of Correct Dress* (New York: London, 1914)

Worth Jean-Philippe, *A Century of Fashion* (Boston, 1928)

Worthy, James C., *Shaping an American Institution: Robert E. Wood and Sears, Roebuck and Company* (Urbana, Illinois, 1984)

Wyndham Horace, *Chorus to Coronet* (London, 1951)

Ziegfeld, Richard E., *The Ziegfeld Touch: The Life and Times of Florenz Ziegfeld, Jr* (New York, 1993)

Magazines, newspapers and directories

The Bystander

Chicago Daily Tribune

The Court Journal

Everywoman's Encyclopaedia

Femina

Good Housekeeping (Holyoke, Mass. and New York)

The Graphic

Harper's Bazaar

The Illustrated London News

L'Illustration

The Lady

The Lady's Realm

Lake Side Directory of Chicago, 1915–19 (telephone directory)

London Post Office Directories

Les Modes

The New York Times

The New York American Examiner

The Play Pictorial

The Queen

The Saturday Evening Post

The Sketch

The Smart Set. A Magazine of Cleverness (New York and London)

The Sunday Express (London)

The Tatler

The Theatre Magazine

The Times

Vanity Fair

The Washington Post

The Woman at Home

Notes

INTRODUCTION

[1] Peel (1933), p.67

[2] Duff Gordon (1932)

[3] *The New York American Examiner*, 1910

[4] Pearce (1993), p.55

[5] Letter from Lucy Duff Gordon to the Curator, The Museum of London, 22 May 1928

[6] *The New York American Examiner,* 1910

CHAPTER ONE '…MOST BEWITCHING GOWNS…' 1890-1905

[1] *The Queen*, 12 April 1902

[2] *The New York American Examiner*, 13 March 1910

[3] *The Queen*, 10 February 1894, and *Why Dressmaking does not Pay, and the Dressmaker's Future*, a pamphlet by 'Scissors', June 1895

[4] Duff Gordon (1932), p.54

[5] Glyn, Elinor, *Romantic Adventure* (1936), p.47

[6] Duff Gordon (1932) p.44

[7] Glyn, Elinor, *An Illustrated record of the Gowns of Lucy Wallace and Elinor Sutherland, January 1892*. Manuscript. Private Collection.

[8] *The Court Journal*, 10 July 1897

[9] Forbes (1921), p.79

[10] *The Queen*, 2 June 1894

[11] Post Office London Trades' Directory 1900

[12] Duff Gordon (1932), p.71

[13] *From LUCILE Ltd. Autumn 1905. 23 Hanover Square, London, W.* Album containing 69 watercolour fashion designs, V&A: T.89a–1986. Purchased by the V&A in 1986 with the album *From LUCILE Ltd. Autumn 1904. 23 Hanover Square London W.* V&A: T.89–1986.

[14] Glyn, Elinor, *Romantic Adventure* (1936), p.217

[15] Duff Gordon (1932), p.64

[16] Ribeiro (1984), p.98

[17] Glyn (1936), p.165

[18] Battersea (1922), p.118

[19] Forbes (1921) p.79

[20] *The Lady*, 22 June 1905

[21] Mid-1890s: an *haute couture* Worth evening gown cost 100–150 gns (*Discretions*, Frances, Countess of Warwick, 1931, p.166). July 1899: in Paris, with its protectionist regime, a modest dress allowance was £100; a custom-made tailored costume cost £16–25, and an afternoon dress £20–30 (*The Woman at Home*). February 1900: in London, an evening gown of real lace and chiffon cost 30gns and a readymade gown or 'reach me down' cost 5gns (*The Lady's Realm*). 1900–1: Maud Cassel was reputed to have spent £5,000 on her trousseau. 1902: a well-dressed society lady could barely manage with a dress allowance of £200 a year (excluding furs and riding habits) and a minimal annual allowance was £50 (Mrs Eric Pritchard, *The Cult of Chiffon*, pp.128–9).

[22] 'The Decay of Home Life in England', *The Lady's Realm,* February 1903

[23] Benkovitz, M.J., *Ronald Firbank: A Biography* (1970)

[24] Mrs Mason, New Burlington Street: a successful court dressmaker, popular for presentation and wedding 'picture gowns', theatrical and fancy dress. Madame Kate Reily, Dover Street: a leading court dressmaker and milliner noted for ephemeral gowns in chiffons and silks; she also imported clothes from Paris.

[25] Wharton (1934), p.146

[26] Duff Gordon (1932), p.79

[27] Peel (1933), p.47

[28] Duff Gordon (1932), p.45

[29] Sermoneta (1929) p.93

[30] Countess de la Warr, 'The Art of Dressing Well' in *The Lady's Realm*, August 1900

[31] 'Fashion v Hygiene', letter to the Editor from F. May Dickenson Berry MD, in *The Times,* 13 August 1901

[32] Asquith (1952), p.130

[33] Forbes (1921), p.98

[34] *The Queen,* 13 September 1902

[35] Pritchard, Mrs Eric, *The Cult of Chiffon* (1902), p.30. Lucile borrowed the name 'The Cult of Chiffon' for Suggestion 11 in her private view of 'Costume Suggestions', April 1904.

[36] Pless (1929)

[37] Balsan (1952), p.124

[38] Nicolson Harold, *Small Talk* (1937)

[39] Duff Gordon (1932), p.80

CHAPTER TWO FROM LUCILE LTD. AUTUMN 1905

THE MAKING, MEANING AND BIOGRAPHY OF FROM LUCILE LTD. AUTUMN 1905.

[1] Edwards, Elizabeth, 'Photographs as Objects of Memory', in *Material Memories* (1999), p.22

[2] Bell, S.E., 'Fashion Drawing as a Profession for Women', in *Every Woman's Encyclopaedia* (c.1911), p.2288

[3] Edwards (1999), p.230

[4] 'This is probably the first sale of a library devoted entirely to the study of fashion.' *Christie's International Magazine*, April/May 1986

[5] Rothstein, Natalie (ed.), *Barbara Johnson's Album of Styles and Fabrics* (1987)

[6] Duff Gordon (1932), p.43

'CARRESAUTE', AN EVENING GOWN

[1] Beaton (1954), p.32

[2] The dress was purchased at a 'Passion for Fashion & Fine Textiles' sale, 10 July 2007 (lot no. 71), Kerry Taylor in association with Sotheby's sale. No other dresses were credited to the original wearer. We are most grateful to V&A curator Oriole Cullen.

[3] Duff Gordon (1932), p.245

[4] Duff Gordon, Lucy, 'The Last Word in Fashion', in *Harper's Bazaar*, March 1917, p.74. With thanks to Samantha Erin Safer for generously providing a copy of this article.

[5] 'Lucile finds inspiration in epochs of romance', in American *Vogue*, 1 January 1921, p.32

CHAPTER THREE '…THE RAIMENT OF ALLUREMENT..' 1906-1935

[1] Duff Gordon, Lucy, 'Modes of Today in Tea Apparel', in *Good Housekeeping*, December 1912, p.811

[2] Beaton, Cecil, *The Book of Beauty* (1930), p.18

[3] Asquith (1952), p.75

[4] Peel (1933), p.41

[5] Kaplan and Stowell (1994)

[6] Beaton (1954), p.32

[7] Programme, 'Private View, Friday September 2nd at 5 p.m. at La Salle Lucile', 1904

[8] *The Queen*, September 1904

[9] '*La Sculpture qui bouge*' in Arsène, Alexandre, *Les Reines de l'Aiguille* (1902), p.67

[10] Duff Gordon (1932), p.101

[11] Beaton, Cecil, *The Years Between. Diaries 1939–44* (1965), p.115

[12] *The Times of India,* 27 November 1911

[13] Post, Emily, *Etiquette* (1922, reprinted 1969), p.2

[14] Duff Gordon (1932), p.136

[15] Glyn, Elinor, *Romantic Adventure* (1936), p.151

[16] *The Queen,* 15 April, 1911

[17] Duff Gordon (1932), p.190

[18] 'Pompon' was illustrated in *Fémina,* October 1910, and in *Art et Décoration,* April 1911. A Henri Manuel photograph of 'Isadora' 1910–11 appears in Palmer White's *Poiret* (1973), p.36

[19] Adburgham (1964), p.248

[20] Duff Gordon (1932), p.190

[21] Ibid., p.194

[22] American *Good Housekeeping,* October 1912

[23] *The New York American Examiner,* 13 March 1910

[24] Beaton (1930), p.18

[25] Woolman Chase (1954), pp.98–9

[26] Duff Gordon (1932), p.222

[27] ibid., p.213

[28] The 1915–16 prospectus states that students had designed frocks and hats for Lucile's collections, using American materials. By the academic year 1919–20, Lucile's name is no longer listed. We are most grateful to Caroline Evans for sharing this information.

[29] Greer (1952), p.40

[30] Duff Gordon (1932), p.214

[31] ibid., pp.213–14

[32] Woolman Chase (1954) pp.98–109

[33] For photographs from the *Flower* pageant, see British *Vogue,* Late August 1917, p.14.

[34] Greer (1952), p.41

[35] ibid.

[36] British *Vogue,* early March 1917, p.27

[37] On the 90th anniversary of the case, a two-day conference was held at the New York State Judicial Institute at Pace University School of Law to examine the legal issues in what the programme described as '…one of the most enduring and influential cases in the contracts pantheon'.

[38] Leese (1976), p.12. Leese states that the 7th, 9th and 11th editions of this cultural review show featured Lucile and her designs. By 1919 the show became a fashion feature and Lucile appeared so frequently that it prompted the parody 'Lady Muff Boredom', published in the *Transatlantic Screen Magazine* (no. 164). Unfortunately, the British Film Institute does not house the original footage.

[39] Fashion Institute of Technology, *Designing the It Girl: Lucile and her Style,* catalogue entry 44.

[40] This was reported on pp.816–17. For other weddings that Lucile dressed see, for example, *The Queen,* 23 February 1918, p.215 and 23 March 1919, p.313.

[41] Duff Gordon (1932) p.224

[42] The name on the album cover is spelt 'Thompson', but it is written 'Tompson' on the reverse of the photographs, which was probably contemporaneous and more likely to be correct. Other items ordered were an embroidered and fur-trimmed layered silk dress; a floral printed shepherdess-style dress; a pearl-embroidered filmy silk evening dress; a silk satin coat trimmed with kolinsky fur and matching high-buttoning under-blouse; a silk opera coat with caped shoulder and low-cut, wide sleeves with banded fur.

[43] Duff Gordon (1932), p.259

[44] Greenwall, H.J., 'How Lucile Launches a New Fashion' in the *Sunday Express,* 7 September 1919, p.5

[45] 'Lady (Lucy) Duff-Gordon's Bankruptcy' in *The Times,* 19 April 1923, p.5

[46] Shulhof is listed as 'Director' in the company records dated 3 July 1919

[47] Greer (1952), p.74

[48] Molyneux is listed as a shareholder in the company records.

[49] British *Vogue,* late January 1920, p.40

[50] British *Vogue,* October 1920, p.50

[51] American *Vogue,* 1 January 1921, p.32

[52] *The Times,* 15 February 1923, p.5

[53] Unattributed newspaper article from the archive at FIT. We thank Caroline Evans for this reference.

[54] *The Times,* 15 February 1923, p.5

[55] *The Times,* 19 April 1923, p.5

[56] Hartnell (1954), p.23

[57] Ibid.

[58] Memorandum and Article of Association of Lucy Duff Gordon Ltd

[59] Warwick, Frances, Countess of, *Discretions* (1931), p.165

[60] Winding-up records of Lucy Duff Gordon Ltd

APPENDICES

LUCILE ARCHIVE

[1] 'Lady Duff Gordon Talks of Fashions', unattributed article 1911, Box 15, Lucile Archive, Special Collections, Gladys Marcus Library, Fashion Institute of Technology, New York. Thank you to Caroline Evans.

LUCILE LTD IN BRITISH COLLECTIONS

[1] Benkovitz, Miriam J., *Ronald Firbank: A Biography* (1970), p.269. His papers are housed in the New York Public Library.

[2] V&A registered papers.

[3] Telegraph.co.uk, 15 January 2006.

Index

Figures in *italics* refer to captions

Afterword

The authors pass the final words to Lucile, who, in the concluding passage of her autobiography, was emphatic that while not a 'slavish admirer of the past… I do regret the passing of so much of the romance which made the world a very pleasant place… . It is possible to look upon realities too much, so that you lose the power of make-believe, and I think that perhaps is a mistake which we are all making to-day.'